THE Jacob FORD JR. MANSION

THE Jacob FORD JR. MANSION

The Storied History OF A NEW JERSEY HOME

Jude M. Pfister

Published by The History Press
Charleston, SC 29403
www.historypress.net

First published 2009

Library of Congress CIP data applied for.

Notice: The information in this book is true and complete to the best of our knowledge. It is offered without guarantee on the part of the author or The History Press. The author and The History Press disclaim all liability in connection with the use of this book.

To my wife,
Miriam

Contents

Contents

Acknowledgements

This book would not have been possible without the many dedicated professionals working for the National Park Service in the field of resource preservation. It is their collective works I turned to over and over for information in writing what is admittedly a work of synthesis. I'm not claiming much originality beyond stitching together the various threads that they wrote separately as reports commissioned for specific reasons. Their works more times than not suffered the fate of many specialty reports: sequestration to a shelf to spend its life collecting dust. If they were ever utilized, it was not by the public. Therefore, this book should be seen as an attempt to provide an overview of the topics covered. In no way should it be considered "definitive." Its purpose is to inspire others to further research.

Acknowledgement must first be made for Randy Turner, superintendent of the Morristown National Historic Park, who agreed to let me take time to work on this project. My curatorial colleague Joni Rowe provided many leads and ideas. Krystal Poelstra patiently provided research and technical assistance. Those who have read the manuscript and offered criticism and editing have made the book more readable and more compelling as a story. They include Judy Jacobs, Debbie Van Buren, Anne DeGraaf and Gordon Ward. Their insight and careful judgment have prevented many errors. What errors that slipped past their keen eyes are mine and mine alone. Thanks are also due to the professional staff at The History Press who knowledgably took words on paper and produced a book. I must also thank those who will remain nameless who offered encouragement during the tedious hours of writing and research. I have a great debt of gratitude to repay to them someday.

CHAPTER 1

Introduction

The Purpose of this Book

This book is a biography of a house. It presents the history of a structure that has been important since its construction began in 1772. The history of that importance is a story of human proportions, which played out in the house known as the Ford Mansion, the subject of this book.

American history is rarely approached through the witness or the perspective of a tangible structure. But when it is, historic structures often "talk" about how they have changed over time, if we listen. Normally, a tour guide provides a narrative of a historic home and the story it has to tell for visitors. In many cases, the guide will rely on a script composed of multiple parts drawn from many different independent studies of the structure and its story. By itself, though, the structure does allow you to observe for yourself the story it has to tell. Through observation and a little knowledge, many visitors can see beyond the layers to the multiple stories that lie beneath the surface. Rarely is the past so far removed from a building, particularly a historic home. Historic structures of all types are known for revealing their secrets to those who are knowledgeable enough, and willing, to discern the signs. It is as though a structure never completely allows itself over time to be so fully renovated that we cannot understand what it is trying to tell us. No matter how hard future generations try, they can never cover over every item of evidence (short of demolition) of past occupation. There will always be some element or layer of those who lived or worked in the structure before us.

It is easy to look at a structure in human terms. This book seeks to portray the Ford Mansion as a character in the narrative equal to the personalities who occupied it. When discussing a structure in terms of human qualities, it is sometimes forgotten that we are, after all, discussing an inanimate object. An inanimate object does not necessarily relate to us in any cognitive, meaningful way. The best way a house can relate to us is by representing the owner. Many times, houses reflect or convey the attitude or status of the owner. Homes advertise to observers and visitors the qualities that the owner holds high. In this way, the house does speak to us. The symbolic and emotional ties we create with the physical structure allow us to "hear" ourselves as part of material reality. Still, it is difficult to approach an object of such antiquity as the Ford Mansion (as understood in American terms) without a sort of reverence. There is an element of respect that we feel is naturally due to an object, any object, that survives for such an extended period of time. We like to quote the phrase "respect your elders." In many ways, this admonition is as appropriate for historic sites as it is for historic figures. Time knows no boundary between animate and inanimate. That is why we have a natural reverence for the past and why historic sites are so intrinsically important.

In one sense, the layers of history in a historic house are like the stanzas of a poem. The historic house becomes the poet of the past, capable of evoking a variety of epochs relating to its past. As the poet Henry Wadsworth Longfellow wrote, "All houses wherein men have lived and died Are haunted houses."[1] Longfellow—who himself lived in a historic mansion in Cambridge, Massachusetts, that was once also occupied by Washington—gives voice to the many layers of history that, when combined, present us with a story. For Longfellow, historic houses, or any old structure, never lose the associations they have had, regardless of how much time has passed. In his poem, Longfellow was also writing in part to remind Americans that they, too, have a past, something that can be revered and honored or reviled, as the case may be.

Knowing how a structure was utilized tells us much about those individuals who have preceded us in the historical timetable. Whether famous or not, people have all left their mark. Over time, historic houses are generally updated to the latest architectural fashion; their occupants can participate in the great events of the day; and the house can even serve as a setting for history more than once. Through it all, though, the structure remains a guide to the past. The one unending tangible symbol of the past, however altered, is the structure itself.

Introduction

THE MANSION'S IMPORTANCE

Aside from the fact that the Jacob Ford Jr. Mansion was host to George Washington during a winter encampment in 1779–80, it still has a story to tell beyond that event and is still an invaluable source for understanding the past. Even if the Washington connection did not exist, the social implications alone for the Ford Mansion history would make it an important building. The social aspects of the mansion's construction occurred nearly a decade before Washington arrived, when the wealth of the Ford family allowed them to boldly take a stand in the community as leaders and decision makers by building the mansion. The fact that Washington occupied the mansion in 1779–80 simply added another layer to an already rich story in terms of the overall history of the Ford Mansion.

Prior to Washington's arrival in 1779, the mansion was the scene of great human tragedy for the Ford family. Before 1779, when Washington arrived, the mansion had already briefly played host to Continental soldiers in the abbreviated 1777 encampment. The presence of such an enormous historical figure as Washington should not be allowed to overshadow the significant story that this structure, or any structure, has witnessed through direct participation in great national events. Furthermore, even if a house is not a direct participant in large historical events, houses, through more indirect observation of events over the years, can lend to the overall aspect of American history by simply surviving all the potentially disastrous events that time can visit on a structure.[2]

The Jacob Ford Jr. family (no relation to other famous Fords such as the automobile mogul Henry Ford or President Gerald Ford) built the mansion between 1772 and 1774 using proceeds from their successful iron business. While the mansion is of grand proportions, it lacks some aspects associated with showcase homes of the period. Intricate decorative embellishments are not apparent inside the house, and the exterior lacks some of the appointments found on houses of similarly financially empowered families of the time period. This lack of ostentation is generally attributed to the Presbyterian faith of the Ford family, which traditionally eschewed displays of wealth. Another possibility is that Jacob Ford Jr. joined the war effort before the mansion was finished and died before it ended, thus leaving much of the interior incomplete and unsuitable for decorating. At best, though, the family only met this possible religious requirement for unostentatious living halfway, if that indeed moved them. It is impossible to explain away the presence of a mansion; it simply is not a sign of a subdued display of wealth and power.

Dr. The Estate of Jacob Ford Junr. in a/c with the estate of J. Ford Senr.

1777 July 30	To cash paid		Will. D Hart		£12.5.2
" " "	To cash paid		Ebenezer Tuttle		1.15.0
" " "	To	do.	Elij. Leonard		1.18.2
" " "	To	do.	John Herriman		1.15.9
" Augt. 2.	To	do.	Elij. Leonard		13.6.9
" " 12.	To	do.	M. Raynor		11.11.4
" " "	To	do.	D. Anderson		4.4.7
" Octr. 4	To	do.	G. Rapalje		3.11.7
" Novr. 8	To	do.	Revd. T. Johnes to pay Ludlow's bond		164.1.3
" " 22.	To	do.	Jabez Campfield		38.5.7
" Decr. 8	To	do.	Theodosia Ford		106.15.0
1778 Jany. 12.	To	do.	Fred. King		25.10.8
" " 21.	To	do.	Dr. Timo. Johnes		119.5.0
" Feb. 4.	To	do.	Theodosia Ford		289.16.1
" Mar. 3.	To	do.	Jona. Ford		85.9.9
" " 13	To	do.	Benj. Lindsly		222.19.6
" May 2.	To	do.	Theodosia Ford		289.16.1

In the above manner Dr. Tuttle advanced money habitually for the Estate of Jacob Ford Junr. and no doubt but this £1217. was so advanced, & that Moses Tuttle understood it so when it was put into his hands, and never intended otherwise until in Septemr. 1777 it became realized into a specie bond: then he ordered the money, after it

Part of the reconciliation of the estates of the two Jacob Fords, who both died in January 1777. *Morristown National Historical Park.*

The Ford mansion, after Washington, stayed in the Ford family until 1873. It stood through all the trials and tribulations of the growing country. It kept its watch on Morris Avenue during the War of 1812, it saw the first death of an American president in office when William Henry Harrison died in 1841 (it has of course seen every other death of a president in office since then) and it stood through the Mexican War adventures of President Polk, who fully embraced President Monroe's doctrine of Manifest Destiny.

The mansion has withstood numerous national financial crises, ranging from 1837 to 1929 and beyond, and has maintained its dignity through countless national upheavals, good and bad. The mansion, which was built as the nation was first beginning to come together, witnessed nearly the end of all that its builders had hoped for when the nation plunged itself into Civil War. The aspect of the mansion's observation of history unfolding is over 230 years in the making. Needless to say, it has seen, and been through, a lot. Structures and historic sites, and in particular the Ford Mansion, are as much a part of the fabric of history as are the men and women who occupied them.

How We View Importance

The field of historic preservation has immeasurably contributed to the sense of reverence we feel toward the longevity achieved by structures. With the Jacob Ford Jr. Mansion, the assurance of longevity was to a point guaranteed by the six months that Washington used the house as his headquarters during the winter encampment of 1779–80. By the presence of the military leader of the American Revolutionary War effort, the mansion gained a level of importance that would continue to draw attention as the years progressed after the war.

This does not mean that the mansion would not have been a historic portal to a bygone era had Washington not stayed there. The unique element, the nearly overpowering essence of "the power of place," should not be ignored. Without Washington, the mansion would be entirely representative of the social and economic structure of the eighteenth-century America that created it. Without the influx of immigration, the removal of the Indians, exploitable natural resources and slave labor, the Ford Mansion would never have been built. To overlook this is to ignore the larger forces promoting the Revolution in the first place. And the mansion's early years are intimately intertwined with the Revolution.

Without the rapid economic expansion brought about by organized exploitation of the abundant resources available in the colonies, the Revolution may never have occurred. Without the Revolution, Washington would not have occupied the mansion, and without the resources, the mansion may not have existed. Therefore, it is important not to overemphasize only one aspect of history. All elements are important to understanding the full history of a site. History does not exist and did not occur in a vacuum. It cannot consequently be experienced in a vacuum.

The historic preservation movement played a significant role in ensuring that the mansion survived beyond its 100th birthday. In fact, had the motivation for preservation not enveloped the Ford Mansion, it probably would not have survived until the American centennial in 1876. On its own, by 1876, without the Washington connection, the mansion would not have survived the progress of history, regardless of how important it was.

THE FORDS AND HISTORY

This book will also seek to place the Ford Mansion as a building within the context of the larger canvas of New Jersey and American history. The Ford family, the Washington military family, the Washington Association of New Jersey and the American family—as citizens of a nation who collectively maintain the mansion—have all called the mansion "home." It will be the task of this book to integrate the mansion's various aspects of ownership (the Fords, the Washington military family, the Washington Association and the American people) that combined to create the story of this one structure. It would surely be enough to look at each individual unit of ownership over the past 235 years. However, this would only give us one segment of the story. What is called for—what is necessary for the complete, unified story—is an understanding of how each successive "owner" utilized the mansion and was able to evoke a sense of place within the same four walls.

In the following chapters, the familiar and not-so-familiar contours of New Jersey and American history will be presented. In most instances, the narrative will be quite standard in its approach to the general outline of events. However, as one purpose of responsible history is to provide information on less well-known aspects of history, this book will attempt to provide an even larger mosaic in some instances. There are two partial reasons for this: one, the records for the Ford family and the Ford Mansion are minimal. The story must sometimes therefore be created from elsewhere; and two, this approach will allow the reader to enter into—as nearly as possible—the tumultuous times that brought the mansion into existence and beyond.

Finally, in terms of the mansion, there is no way to fully know what it looked like when it was built, when Washington occupied it, when the Ford family maintained it until 1873 and during most of the administration of the Washington Association of New Jersey. What is seen today is the best interpretation of the evidence that has been uncovered over the past seventy-five years since the National Park Service (NPS) acquired the site. Even with that understanding, there are certain elements of the mansion as seen today that simply did not exist in 1779–80. As a brief example, there was no fireplace in the room shown as Washington's office. Closets once existed where shelves are located now in Mrs. Ford's room. There was a door between the conference room and Washington's office. The changes over the years, while subtle in most instances, have created a tableau or stage set of what can only be described as a best-case scenario based in most instances on extensive architectural study.[3] Even this though is not exact, in some cases the evidence leads nowhere, and the issue must be resolved by inference.

Lastly, there is the issue of how unfinished the mansion was in 1777, the year Jacob Ford Jr. died. Some evidence points to a structure barely habitable, while other evidence points to a more completed building. According to the most recent scholarly studies, "[I]t is possible that the mansion had existed in an unfinished state, to whatever extent, for some twenty-four years and was only brought to completion around 1800."[4] The study of the condition of the mansion at the outbreak of the Revolution seems to indicate that Jacob Ford Jr. did indeed leave his mansion as it was and proceeded to take up arms against the British. My discussion here on the mansion is therefore partly inference and partly known fact.

CHAPTER 2

The Ford Family Builds a Home in Colonial New Jersey

A Brief Overview of the Fords of New Jersey

To begin the story of the Ford family and their mansion, it is best to present a brief overview of their varied activities.

The Jacob Ford Jr. family was fully American, albeit colonial, in 1772. The family had ties in the colonies that stretched back over one hundred years. The family appears to have immigrated to the northern New Jersey area from New England in the late seventeenth century, perhaps as a result of the colonization campaign run by the English.[5] The family had settled in New Jersey within the first decade of the eighteenth century and established a family iron forge at Whippany in what became Morris County. The family was drawn to the iron business early and began to flourish by mid-century. Thanks to the prosperity of the iron business, Jacob Ford Sr., like other members of the growing upper class, also became a large landowner by mid-century and was able to deed two hundred acres to his son Jacob Jr. in 1762, the year of Jacob Jr.'s marriage to Theodosia Johnes. This land was part of a family legacy that stretched back to the Fords' first arrival in New Jersey.

Ten years later, in 1772, Ford Jr. would commence to build his family's mansion on a "low Piedmont hill east of the town center and just south of the Whippany river."[6] The 200 acres that Jacob Ford Sr. deeded to his son were well above the average number for a farm in the Morristown area, which averaged around 125 acres.[7] Jacob Ford Sr. had provided his son an estate of considerable size upon his marriage to the daughter of the rector

Land agreement between Jacob Ford Sr. and Jacob Ford Jr., 1774. *Morristown National Historical Park.*

of the Presbyterian Church. Jacob Ford Sr. had acquired the land on which Jacob Ford Jr. built his mansion in 1742, possibly as an investment, as the family at the time lived in nearby Mount Hope.[8]

The Ford family continued to add to their holdings over the decades, and as a result, by the time the mansion was started in 1772, the family was one of the largest landowners in the county. The mansion was situated on the property at the confluence of two major roads connecting the old towns of Elizabethtown and Newark. The mansion was well sited to serve a role as a visual representation of the Ford family's power and influence. The Ford Mansion, however, represented not so much an attempt at portraying the family's wealth in a needlessly extravagant way, but rather the Ford Mansion was designed to identify their status as civil leaders and prominent community participants. The Fords were not interested in displaying their wealth for the simple fact of display. It is no wonder then that the Fords decided to build their mansion not so much to present the family as a commercial force to be dealt with, but rather to identify themselves as leaders and co-workers in the task of creating the Morristown community.

To all Christian People to whom these Presents shall come Greeting Know ye that Jacob Ford Esq of Morristown in the County of Morris and Province of New Jersey Merchant for and in Consideration of five Shillings Current Money of the Province af. at Eight Shill. per Ounce to him in hand paid, the Receipt whereof is hereby Confessed Hath Remised Released and forever Quit Claimed unto Samuel Day of Morristown af.d Yeoman and by these Presents doth fully clearly and absolutely Remise Release and for ever Quit Claim unto the s.d Sam.l Day in his full and Peaceable Possession and Seizin and to his Heirs and assigns for ever all such Right Estate Title interest and Demand whatsoever as he the s.d Jacob Ford ever had now hath or Ought to have of in or to all one certain Tract of Land lying and being in Morristown af.d Beginning at a [illegible] Tree for a Corner from thence running North East Thirty Nine Chains and a Rod and a half to an Elm Tree for a Corner from thence North West [illegible] Rods to a stake for a Corner thence South West Thirty Nine Chains one Rod and an half to a stake, and from [illegible] the place of Beginning Containing Fifty acres of Land besides the usual allowance for Roads, which Tract of Land was conveyed to the s.d Jacob Ford by James Rogers late of Morristown af.d by his Deed Dated August 29. 1738, and which was Conveyed [illegible] James Rogers by the above named Sam.l Day by Deed May 18. 1739. To have and to hold all the above bounded Tract of Land with the Building and Orchard on the same together with all other the Profits Privileges Commodities and appurtenances [illegible] belonging or in any wise appertaining [illegible]

Person or Persons for him or them, or in his or their Names, or in the Name or Right or Stead of any of them Shall or will by any ways or means hereafter have, claim Challenge or Demand any Estate Right Title or Interest in or to the Premises or any part [illegible] every action Estate Right Title Interest [illegible] whatsoever of in or to the Premises and every part and Parcel of the same they and every of them shall be utterly Excluded and barred forever by these Presents. In Witness whereof the s.d Jacob Ford hath hereunto set his hand and Seal this Eighth Day of April in the Twenty Seventh Year of his Majesties Reign King George the Second of Great Britain &c Anno Domini 1754.

Sealed and Delivered in the Presence of
Ezekiel Cheever
Hannah her mark Rogers
Jacob Ford

Above, left: Purchase of land by Jacob Ford Sr., circa 1739. *Morristown National Historic Park.*

Above, right: Manuscript possibly relating to the purchase of land by Jacob Ford Sr., 1754. His wife Hannah witnesses the transaction by placing her mark. *Morristown National Historical Park.*

The Presbyterian church was a bulwark of the Morristown village community. Only one other church, a Baptist denomination, existed in 1772. The Fords were prominent members of the community in terms of church, social and civic responsibilities and had a significant level of leadership in the small town. Morristown itself began as an unplanned community around the Presbyterian church, which was built in 1738–40. The construction of the church was supported by Jacob Ford Sr., although he did not donate land. Ford Sr. did assist, however, in the construction of the steeple by providing money and material.[9] The church was built in a section of land that had originally been part of the parcel of lands controlled by the East Jersey Council of Proprietors.[10] At the time, the village of Morristown had slightly over 100 inhabitants. On the eve of the American Revolution, the village of Morristown had about 250 inhabitants. Morris County had a population of about 10,500 at the time of the outbreak of the Revolution.[11] This number is a tenfold increase from when the county was established in 1739.

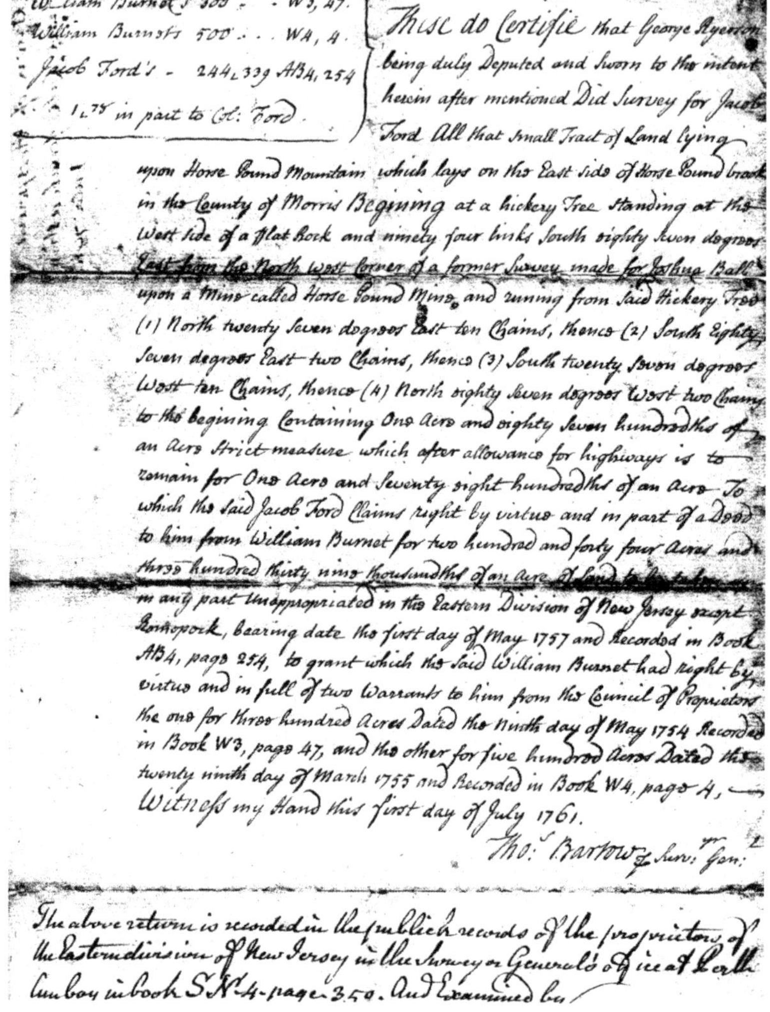

William Burnet's 300 - - W3, 47.
William Burnet's 500 . . . W4, 4.
Jacob Ford's - 244,339 AB4, 254
1,78 in part to Col: Ford.

These do Certifie that George Ryerson being duly Deputed and Sworn to the intent herein after mentioned Did Survey for Jacob Ford All that Small Tract of Land lying upon Horse Pound Mountain which lays on the East side of Horse Pound brook in the County of Morris Begining at a hickory Tree standing at the West side of a flat Rock and ninety four links South eighty seven degrees East from the North west Corner of a former Survey made for Joshua Ball upon a Mine called Horse Pound Mine, and running from said Hickory Tree (1) North twenty Seven degrees East ten Chains, thence (2) South Eighty Seven degrees East two Chains, thence (3) South twenty Seven degrees West ten Chains, thence (4) North eighty Seven degrees West two Chains to the begining Containing One Acre and eighty Seven hundredths of an Acre Strict measure which after allowance for highways is to remain for One Acre and Seventy eight hundredths of an Acre To which the said Jacob Ford Claims right by virtue and in part of a Deed to him from William Burnet for two hundred and forty four Acres and three hundred thirty nine thousandths of an Acre of land to be taken in any part Unappropriated in the Eastern Division of New Jersey except Romopock, bearing date the first day of May 1757 and Recorded in Book AB4, page 254, to grant which the said William Burnet had right by virtue and in full of two Warrants to him from the Council of Proprietors the one for three hundred Acres Dated the ninth day of May 1754 Recorded in Book W3, page 47, and the other for five hundred Acres Dated the twenty ninth day of March 1755 and Recorded in Book W4, page 4, —

Witness my Hand this first day of July 1761.

Thos: Bartow, Survr: Genl:

The above return is recorded in the publick records of the proprietors of the Eastern division of New Jersey in the Surveyor General's office at Perth Amboy in book S No 4 page 350. And Examined by

A 1761 survey of land for Jacob Ford Sr. *Morristown National Historical Park.*

The Morristown area was known as West Hanover and was part of a 5,711-acre area controlled by five members of the council.[12] By 1739, the year when the Presbyterian church was built, Morris County had been created. The provincial legislature had accepted a petition by the leading citizens in the northern part of Hunterdon County to create the new county.[13] Among those citizens signing the petition to form the new county was Jacob Ford Sr. Being approved, the new county would be named Morris, after the governor of the province, Lewis Morris. Morris, who in 1738 had become the first royal governor for New Jersey since 1701, also lent his name to the village of Morristown.[14]

The Fords, Jacob and Theodosia, who married in 1762, had four children survive to adulthood (a fifth child born in the new house died before she was two). Of those who survived, Gabriel, the second eldest, would become the most important in terms of the mansion and maintaining the family property later in his life.

Within quick succession in 1777, Mrs. Ford was dealt several severe blows emotionally. Her husband Jacob Ford Jr., builder of the mansion, died of pneumonia on January 11—at the time of his death, Ford Jr. was a colonel commanding the Morris County militia. Her father-in-law, Ford Sr., died on January 19, just a week later. Several months later in June 1777, her youngest child, a girl, died in the mansion. In addition to all of this, the winter encampment of 1777 in Morristown was taking place. Compounding that event, thirty-five members of the Delaware Light Infantry Regiment, commanded by Thomas Rodney, stayed at the mansion for two weeks, during which time both Jacob Fords passed away. No doubt this was an extremely emotional time for Mrs. Ford. Fortunately, though, "The solid reputation established by her late husband and father-in-law were…[substantial] assets."[15]

Mrs. Ford, only in her late thirties, was left to raise and educate her four remaining children—Timothy, Gabriel, Elizabeth and Jacob III. By the terms of her husband's will, her father-in-law Jacob Ford Sr. was to have received and managed the mansion and the grounds while she was provided the means for the education of the children. Unfortunately, the untimely death of Ford Sr. the same month as his son put a tremendous burden on Mrs. Ford. Upon her father-in-law's death, the property was divided amongst the children, with Mrs. Ford probably acting as guardian for their inheritance until the children reached legal age. The house continued to be jointly owned by the children until Gabriel bought out his brothers and sister in 1805.[16] Mrs. Ford had life tenancy in the mansion, dying there in 1826.

The Colony of New Jersey

The first European settlers in New Jersey (which was not called New Jersey until 1664, although it was divided between East and West Jersey) were Dutch fur traders who lived a precarious existence alongside the indigenous Lenape Indians. Throughout the seventeenth century, only three towns were formally settled. Bergen, later to be known as Jersey City; Elizabethtown; and Newark were all founded in the second half of the century.[17] The Dutch—the term is used to identify Hollanders, Flemings, Protestant French and German speakers—attempted to encourage settlement by recruiting the Swedes and Finns during the seventeenth century, but the Dutch were largely unsuccessful in enticing either the Swedes or the Finns to emigrate.[18]

The English acquired New Jersey and New York from the Dutch in 1664. Charles II granted the area that is today New Jersey to his brother, the Duke of York. In turn, the duke deeded the land to Sir George Carteret and Lord Berkeley in a lease dated June 23, 1664. The duke did, however, exercise his right to name his new territory "New Jersey" in part to honor the Isle of Jersey, which fought for and aided the Royalist cause during the British civil war that restored his brother to the throne as the Stuart monarch Charles II.[19] Elizabethtown was ultimately named for Sir George's wife. This period saw the English attempt, like the Dutch before them, to lure settlers from other colonies by promoting New Jersey as a place with a "favorable degree of self-government, self-taxation, and a limited range of religious freedom."[20] This proved not to be an effective inducement though, and New Jersey lagged behind its neighboring colonies through the early eighteenth century in terms of population development and, consequently, resource development.[21] By 1700, the areas of East and West Jersey were becoming more firmly

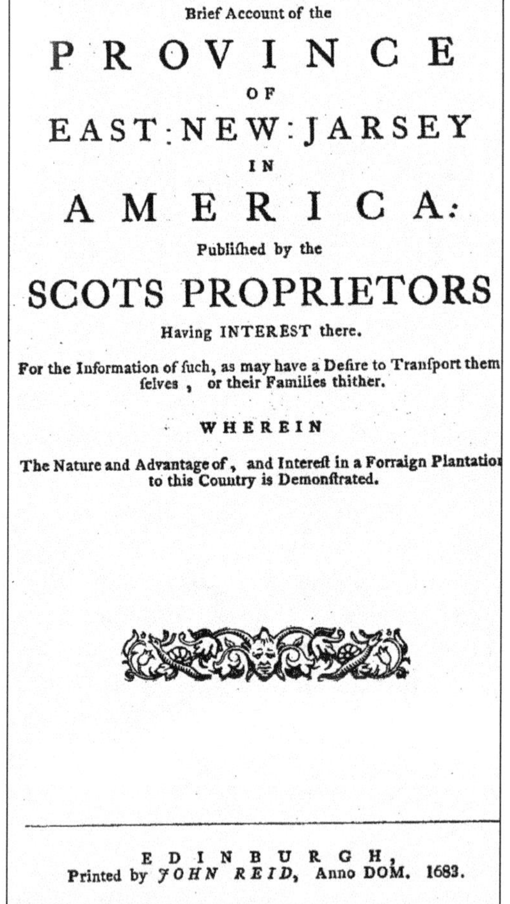
Brief Account of the
PROVINCE
OF
EAST:NEW:JARSEY
IN
AMERICA:
Publiſhed by the
SCOTS PROPRIETORS
Having INTEREST there.
For the Information of ſuch, as may have a Deſire to Tranſport them ſelves , or their Families thither.
WHEREIN
The Nature and Advantage of , and Intereſt in a Forraign Plantatio[n] to this Country is Demonſtrated.

EDINBURGH,
Printed by *JOHN REID*, Anno DOM. 1683.

Title page of narrative depiction of East New Jersey, reprint of 1683 manuscript, 1865. *Morristown National Historical Park.*

For Minerals, It is thought there are not wanting of several sorts, For there is an Iron work already set up, where there is good Iron made; And also, there is discovered already abundance of *Black-Lead*.

It is exceeding well furnished with safe, convenint Harbours, for Shipping, which is of great Advantage, and afords already for exportation, great plenty of Horses, and also Beef, Pork, Pipstaves, Bread, Flower, White, Barly, Rye, *Indian* Corn, Butter, and Cheese, which they export for *Barbadoes*, *Jamaica*, *Mevis*, and other adjacent Islands; As also to *Portugal*, *Spaine*, and the *Canarys*. their *Whale-Oyl*, and *Whale-Fines*, *Beaver*, *Mink*, *Racon*, and *Martine-skins* (which this Countrey produces) they transport for *England*.

The *Indian* Natives in this Countrey are but few, Comparative to the Neighbouring Collony, And these that are there, are so from being formidable, and injurious to the Planters, and Inhabitants, that they are really serviceable, and advantagious to them, not only in hunting, and taking the Deer, and all other wild Creatures, and catching of Fish, and Fowl fit for food, in their seasons; but in the killing and destroying of Bears, Wolves, Foxes, and other Vermine; whose skins and furrs they bring the *English*, and sell at less pryce, then the value of time that people must spend to take them. Like as, that this Collony may be founded in Justice, and without any thing of Oppression, as all that is already Planted, is truely Purchassed from the *Indians*, so there is a great deal more of the Province cleared by their consent, and all is intended by paction with them to be obtained, so that whoever Purchase, or Plant under the Proprietors, shal be fred of that incumbrance; and if there were any

The Proprietors have framed a new Schem of Government, which is not yet fully concluded one, but is intended rather to be an enlarging, than an abbreviating of the former, and making it more easie, and advantagious for the Inhabitants, the Chief parts of it are;

That the 24. Proprietors shall chuse a Governour, 16. of them has a Conclusive Vote in it, after the death of him now chosen, he shall continue but for 3. years, and be lyable to the Censure of the Proprietors, and great Counsel, and punishable if he transgress. There is a great Counsel to meet once a year (and sit, if they see meet, for 3. Moneths) consisting of the 24. Proprietors, and 48. chosen by the Planters, and Inhabitants, two thirds Conclude, the one half of the Proprietors assenting; and no money can be raised, or Law made, to touch any mans Libertie or Property, but by this Counsel. There is a Common Counsel to sit constantly, Consisting of the 24. Proprietors, or their Proxies, and nine chosen out of the Representatives of the Planters, in all 33. to be divided into three Commities; 11. to each, one for the Publick Policie: One for the Treasurie and Trade, and one for Plantations.

To aviod Lording over one another, No Man can purchase above the 24th. part of the Countrey; And on the other hand, least any should squander away their Interest, and yet retain the Character of the Government, that belongs to Property, and thence be capable to betray it, as not being bound by Interest, there must be a suteable quanity retained, otherwise the Title in the Government extinguishes in him, and passes to another, to be Elected by the Proprietors, that *Dominion* may follow *Property* and the inconveniency of a *beggarly Nobility*, and *Gentry* may be avoided.

Narrative depiction of East New Jersey, reprint of 1683 manuscript, 1865. *Morristown National Historical Park.*

entrenched in their own identities rather than coming together to form one colony. As has been written, "Above all, the geographic, political, and economic division between East and West Jersey was intensified."[22] Part of this intensification was due to the recruitment polices of the separate regions. East and West Jersey targeted specific cultural groups, which ultimately affected the identities of the two regions.[23]

Although New Jersey was thus nominally split socially, culturally, economically and politically by the boundary line of Sir George and Lord Berkeley, it nonetheless came under the control of Queen Anne in 1702 as a Royal colony irrespective of east and west designations. The proprietors formed a company in the seventeenth century, purchased Native American land titles and distributed its holdings to shareholders.[24] Rather than govern themselves as two separate political entities, the proprietors of both East and West New Jersey decided to unify the colony politically under the British monarchy. Even after this assumption by the Crown, the proprietors still held their respective land titles. This action effectively ended control of the area by the Duke of York and his successors. Furthermore, the proprietors were given governmental control of the colony through an appointed council; they would wield this power until the Revolution.

About 1700, farmers began to move more aggressively into the eastern areas of the colony. "East Jersey, dominated by descendants from New England who migrated into the area in the seventeenth century, was a dynamic region of 'trade, individualism, [and] town meetings,' where a growing, diverse population of English, Dutch, Flemish, and Scotch settlers lived side by side."[25] The Morris County area was known for good soil, water power and forests. Most importantly, the area had rich deposits of iron ore.[26]

New Jersey Iron

Aside from agriculture, the iron industry provided a much-needed source of revenue for Morris County and in some instances created great wealth for a handful of investors and owners like Jacob Ford Sr., who had forges at Mount Pleasant and Speedwell Pond, among other locations. In certain areas, iron production was quite large: "[T]he iron business in Morris County grew until by the time of the American Revolution there were three blast furnaces in operation and over forty forges."[27] The area along the Whippany River seems to have been the focus of the earliest settlements in Morris County due to the nearby gristmills, sawmills, and iron forges.[28]

There is evidence that John Ford, grandfather of the builder of the mansion, had a functioning forge in operation by 1716 in the Morris County area, although he was better known as a carpenter. This was by no means the first forge in the area, as records indicate a forge in New Jersey to have been operating as early as 1685.[29] A further impetus to the iron industry in New Jersey was the passage of the Iron Act of 1750 by the British Parliament. The act removed all duties on pig iron shipped from America to Britain. This act proved imminently beneficial in supporting the New Jersey industry. While records indicate that New Jersey sent relatively little iron overseas, the act nonetheless insured a market should domestic consumption falter.[30]

The early 1740s, when the county was created, coincides with an increase in the number of forges operating in the area. This increase in business must have greatly benefited the Ford family. In fact, given the size of his operation

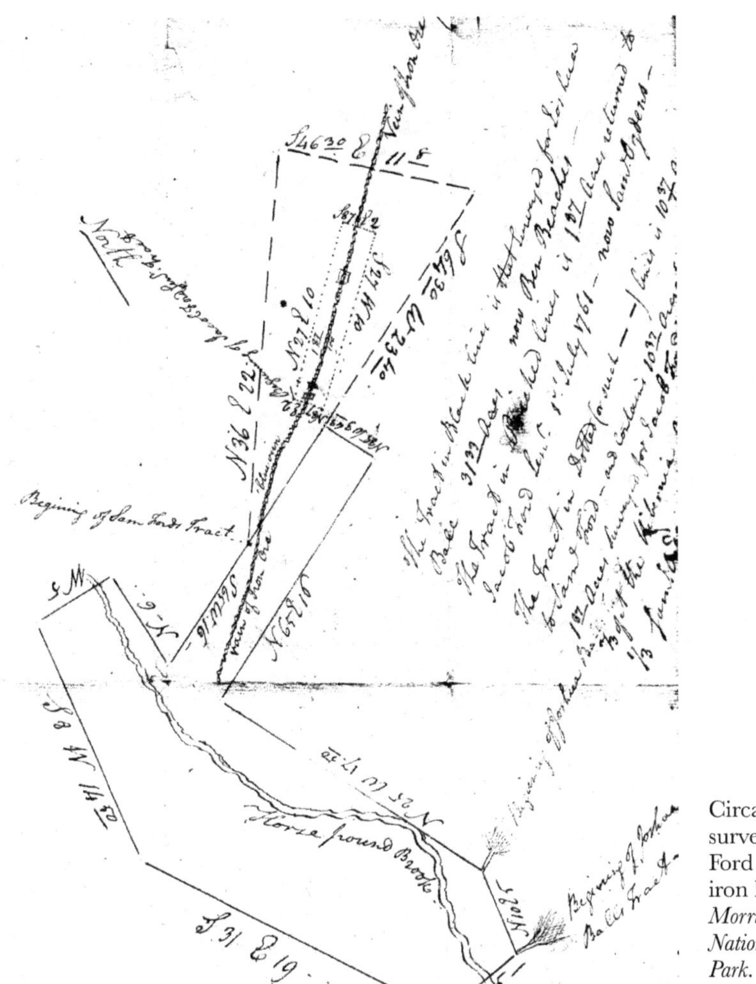

Circa 1776 survey showing Ford family iron holdings. *Morristown National Historical Park.*

and the accumulating wealth, entrepreneurs like "Jacob Ford [who] were *owners* [italics added] of large iron works…hired bloomers and foundry men and may not themselves have known much about actual iron making."[31] The fact that certain individual owners had businesses large enough to hire help was significant. It shows that a labor force could be maintained beyond the self-employment realm. Working for someone, rather than being self-employed, indicates an economy, however small, which can support hired labor in a manufacturing business.

Next to agriculture, the iron industry was infused in every facet of the economic and, thus, the social life in northern New Jersey. The imposing of a business class on the traditional social patterns of agriculture created a

[illegible] his Indenture made the Third day of September in the Th[illegible] Year of the Reign of our [illegible]
[illegible] George the second over Great Britain &c King Anno dom one Thousand Seven Hundred and Thirt[illegible]
[illegible]een John Crane of the township of Hannover in the County [illegible] [illegible]terdon and Western Divisio[illegible]
[illegible]ovince of New Jersey yeoman of the one part and [illegible] [illegible]ship of Hannover and Count[illegible]
[illegible]oman of the other part Witnesseth that the [illegible] the Consent of and good Liking
[illegible]annah his wife for and in consideration of the sum of [illegible] Current Money of this [illegible]
[illegible] him in hand paid by the sd John Crane the Receipt whereof [illegible] sd Jacob Ford Doth here[illegible]
[illegible]

Indenture between John Crane and Jacob Ford Sr. circa 1730. *Morristown National Historical Park.*

societal atmosphere where the contours of money determined the leading citizens. Given the success of their iron business, the Fords clearly enjoyed considerable stature to the extent that the Morristown mansion was not only possible financially, but also accepted by the other residents who participated in the society that recognized such displays of wealth.

The Morris County area developed much like the surrounding areas in terms of agriculture being the predominate source of income for residents. The iron industry provided a supplement, although it peaked with agriculture during the decade before the Revolution. Morristown could boast a diversified economy, thanks in part to the iron industry, composed of lumber, textile and grain processing.[32] "In addition to iron, magnetite, graphite, mica, limestone, and quartz were also mined…A list of taxable property in the township of Morris in 1779 indicates that the town then featured seven saw mills, six gristmills, four tan yards, and seven forges, but no furnaces."[33] Within Morris County however, there were three blast furnaces and over forty forges.[34]

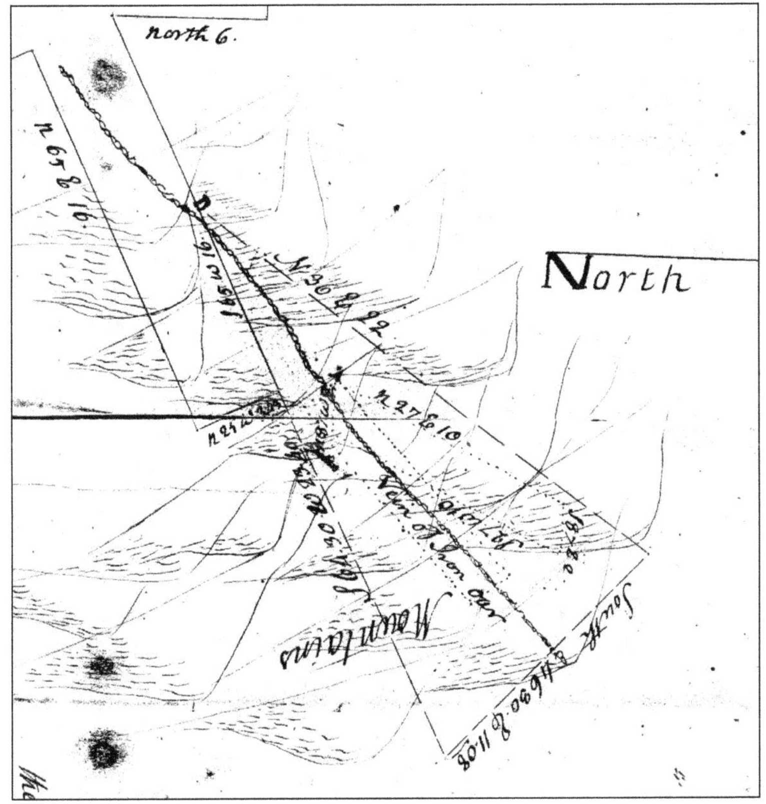

Above: Detail of a map showing the location of a vein of iron ore on Ford property (though not in Morristown), circa 1775. *Morristown National Historical Park.*

Left: The price of iron during various years, with some testimonials about a Ford business associate, Moses Tuttle, circa 1780. *Morristown National Historical Park.*

THE MANSION

In 1762, the commencement exercise at the College of New Jersey featured a hugely patriotic musical entitled *The Military Glory of Great Britain.*[35] Jerseymen, as well as all of British colonial North America, were enjoying a period of triumph, as Britain had defeated France in the struggle for empire in North America. England had a new king, George III; New Jersey had a new governor, William Franklin; and prosperity seemed without end. Both new leaders were young and energetic and exuded an imperial confidence. A year later in 1763, the Treaty of Paris formerly ended the Seven Years' War. William Franklin, son of the famed inventor, would serve as Royal governor of New Jersey longer than any of his colleague governors. He was finally forced from his post in December 1775, long after other Royal governors had left their posts. His imprisonment in Connecticut was approved by the Provincial Congress, the Continental Congress and, unfortunately, his father.

Few could have imagined that as they celebrated in Princeton in 1762 that the incipient strains of imperial destruction were already taking shape. Within ten years, the College of New Jersey at Princeton would be the scene of acts of rebellion that would have been unthinkable in 1763. Within twenty years, a new Treaty of Paris would have Great Britain on the losing side and France the victors via proxy. All in all, events proved quite fluid during the 1760s, and it would have seemed difficult to actually make major long-term plans.

The year 1772, then, might not have seemed the best for a colonial American to celebrate his family's business success by building a large new home. By 1772, one year before the Boston Tea Party, the colonies had already faced the Proclamation Act, the Sugar Act, the Quartering Act, the Stamp Act and the Townshend Act. The Stamp Act marked the "first time Americans had gathered together to discuss common imperial problems and acted in concert to oppose alleged infringements of their freedoms."[36] The Stamp Act Congress declared the act "unconstitutional" and vowed resistance "by all lawful measures."[37] The use of the word "unconstitutional" is very important in that it occurred so early and fell out of use by the time of armed conflict. The rapidity with which patriotism of the early 1760s was replaced with near subversion of the mid-1760s was staggering. Yet, when the Stamp Act was repealed, New Jerseyans celebrated not just the repeal but the birthday of King George III, too.[38]

In 1772, Jacob Ford Sr. was elected to the Colonial Assembly during what was surely a trying period.[39] Two years later, in 1774, the First Continental Congress would meet in Philadelphia. All told, though, 1772, with its vast

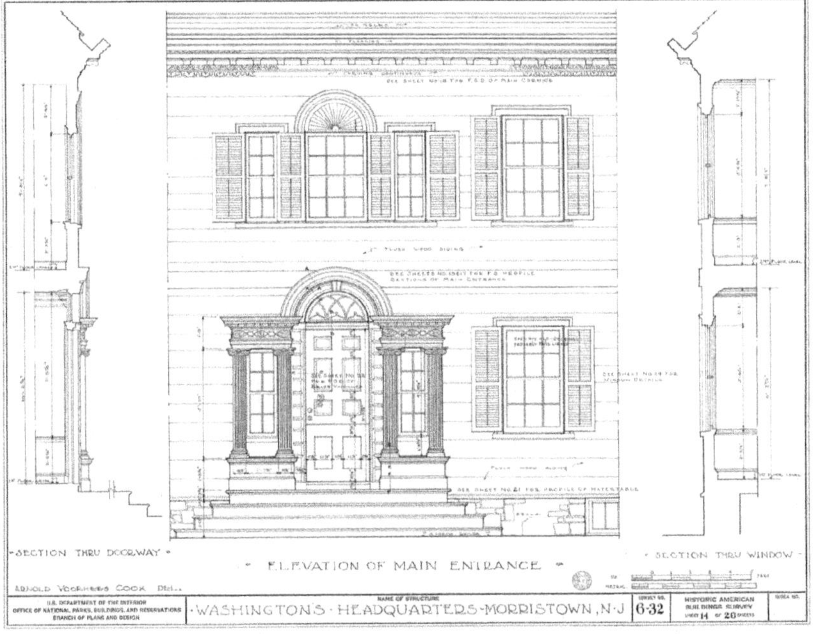

Measured detail drawing of the entrance elevation of the Ford Mansion, 1939. *Historic American Buildings Survey.*

political uncertainties, was not the most auspicious year to embark on a major building project, particularly one designed to establish a home. Yet that is exactly what Jacob and Theodosia Ford did between 1772 and 1774. As the turmoil between Great Britain and the colonies spiraled out of control, the Fords established themselves in a grandly simple, unadorned Georgian-style mansion in Morristown, New Jersey.

In addition to his efforts in Morristown to build the mansion, Jacob Ford Jr. was simultaneously involved with trying to lease another family home nearby. Ford Jr. was responsible for what is today known as the Ford-Faesch House, which was built only a few years before the Morristown mansion. This could account for why there are striking similarities between the two structures. The builder of record for this first home is Jacob Ford Jr., and he did not occupy the home more than three years. It was advertised for lease in 1770 and was leased for twenty-one years to John Jacob Faesch, who took not only the house but also the iron mine and seven hundred acres. This transfer occurred in 1773 while the mansion in Morristown was still under construction.[40] Presumably the family had other lodgings, or the mansion was finished enough to live in.

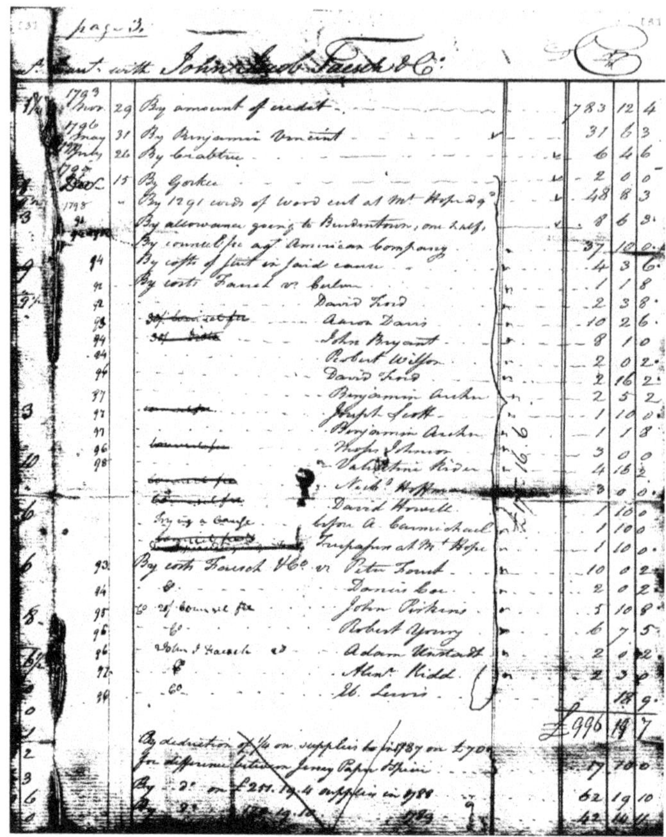

page 3.

Account with John Jacob Faesch & Co.

			£	s	d
1793 Nov.	29	By amount of credit	783	12	4
1796 May	31	By Benjamin Vincent	31	6	3
July	26	By Crabtree	6	4	6
1797 Dec.	15	By Gorkee	2	0	0
1798		By 1291 cords of wood cut at Mt. Hope	48	8	3
94		By allowance going to Burlington, one half	8	6	3
		By counsel fee agt. American company	37	10	0
94		By costs of suit in said cause	4	3	6
91		By costs Faesch vs. [illegible]	1	1	8
92		David Ford	2	3	8
93		Aaron Davis	10	2	6
94		John Bryant	8	1	0
94		Robert Willson	2	0	2
94		David Ford	2	16	2
97		Benjamin Archer	2	5	2
97		Joseph Scott	1	10	0
97		Benjamin Archer	1	1	8
96		Thomas Johnson	3	0	0
98		Valentine Rider	4	16	2
		Nicholas Hoffman	3	0	0
		David Howell	1	10	0
		Trying a cause upon A. Carmichael	1	10	0
		Trespass at Mt. Hope	1	10	0
93		By costs Faesch & Co. vs. Peter Stout	10	0	2
94		Daniel Cox	2	0	2
95		John Perkins	5	10	8
96		Robert Young	6	7	5
96		Adam Umstadt	2	0	2
97		Alexr. Kidd	2	3	0
98		W. Lewis		18	9
			£996	19	7
		By deduction of 1/4 on supplies to 1787 on £70 for difference between Jersey Paper & Specie	17	10	0
		By do. on £251.19.4 supplies in 1788	62	19	10
		By do. on [illegible] 1789	42	14	4

Left: Page of account book of John Jacob Faesch, circa 1795. *Morristown National Historical Park*.

Below: Signature of John Jacob Faesch as witness, circa 1786. *Morristown National Historical Park*.

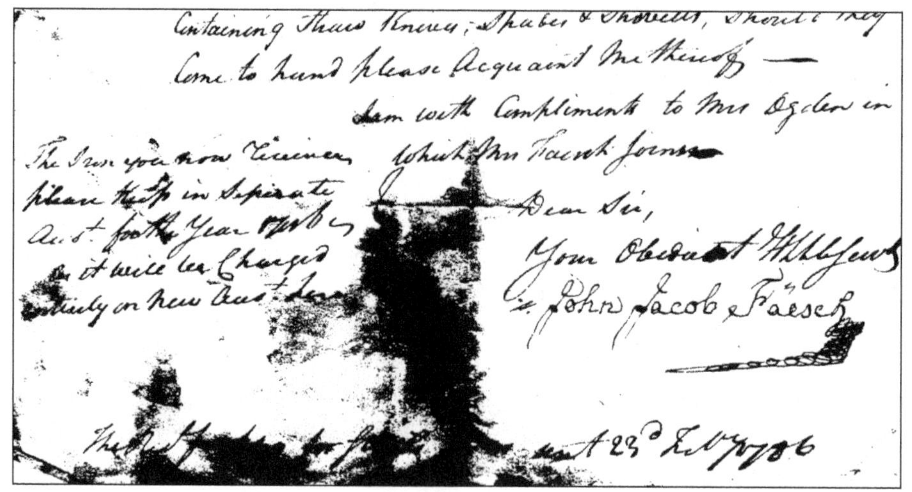

Containing Three Knives, Spades & Shovells, Should they
Come to hand please Acquaint Me thereof —
I am with Compliments to Mrs Ogden in
which Mrs Faesch Joins
Dear Sir,
Your Obedient Hble Servt
John Jacob Faesch

The Iron you now Receive
please Keep in Seperate
Acct for the Year 1786
or it will be Charged
entirely on new Acct

[illegible] 23d Feby 1786

As a merchant and business owner in the iron ore trade, Jacob Ford Jr. had considerable financial resources and social standing with which to build his family a stylish Georgian mansion. With a typical four-room over four-room design floor plan, the main house is architecturally indistinguishable from hundreds of other Georgian houses already built by the early 1770s in the colonies.[41] Overall, "The Ford Mansion represents hybrid architecture: while often described as 'Georgian' for its exterior appearance and internal plan of the house, the presence of the kitchen wing and aspects of its framing show a Dutch influence."[42] The kitchen wing, with its prominent masonry bake oven with spherical top, was constructed at the same time as the rest of the house.

What is significant, though, about the Fords' new house is that the interior first-floor public spaces—the dining room, the parlor and hallway—are all quite simple. While many of the academic architectural elements defining style and class exist in the mansion—"The symmetrical plan and fenestration…and modillion cornice are Georgian"[43]—the decorative elements, which embellish the style and class, do not exist.[44] The two most distinguishing features that allowed guests to know they were in the home of someone with means were the sheer size of the building and the ornate entryway that was as sophisticated as any existing at that time. The entry doorway incorporates many of the features associated with very high-end architecture during the eighteenth century.

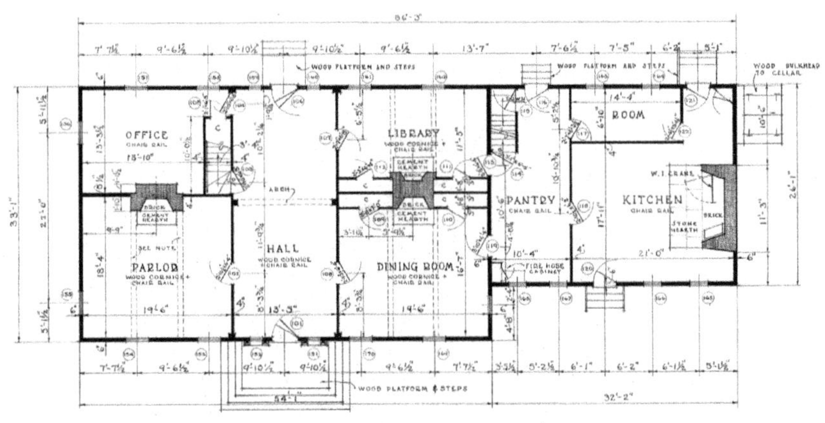

· FIRST · FLOOR · PLAN ·

Measured detail drawing of the first floor of the Ford Mansion, 1939. *Historic American Building Survey*.

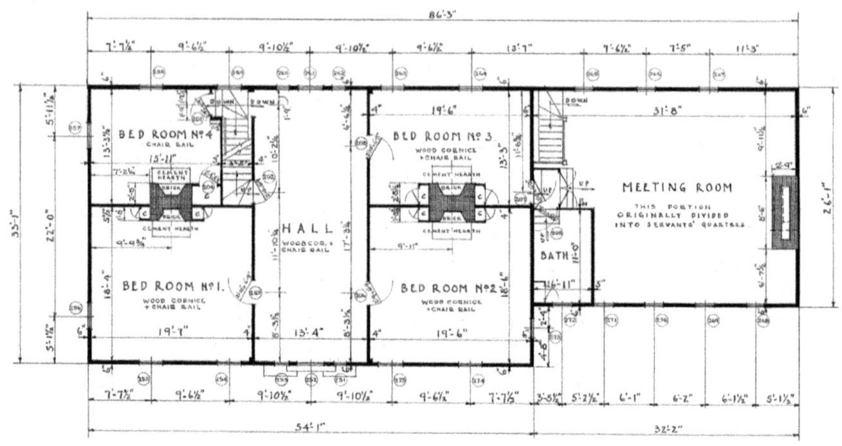

· SECOND · FLOOR · PLAN ·

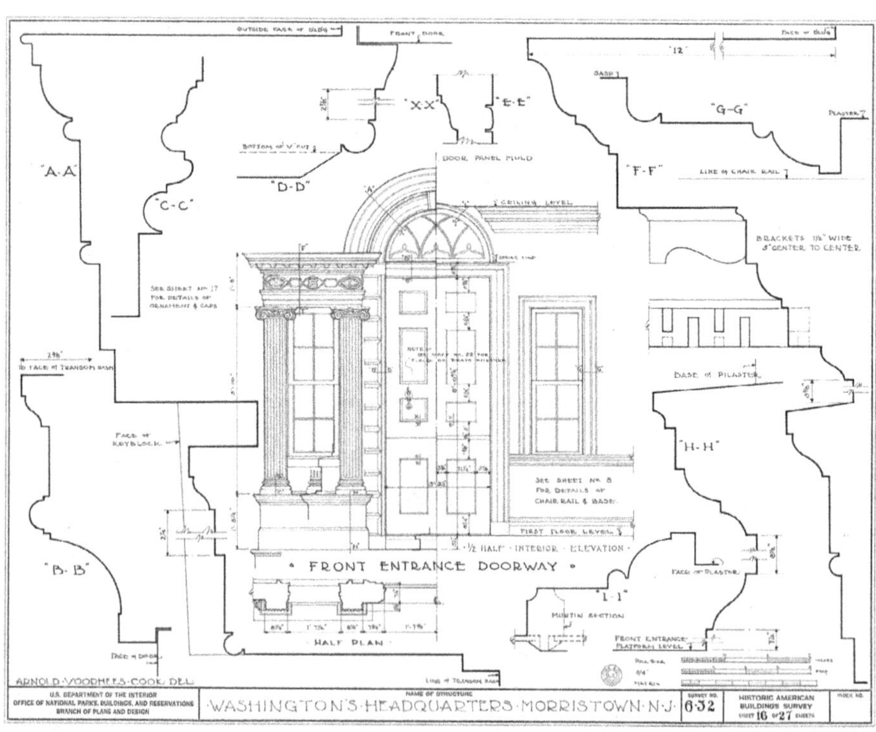

Top: Measured detail drawing of the second floor of the Ford Mansion, 1939. *Historic American Buildings Survey.*

Bottom: Measured detail drawing of the front entrance of the Ford Mansion, 1939. *Historic American Buildings Survey.*

Approaching the front stairs, guests quickly identify the most striking feature as the Palladian entry and window above. The door is flanked by two sidelights, each framed by imposing fluted pilasters with Ionic capitals. The entablature of the entry is composed of a Greek key scroll, dentils and a cornice. The entry is elevated as an architectural necessity, but it nonetheless ensures that all who enter have to look up. Directly above the entryway is a Palladian window at the second floor, designed to continue the grand elements of the front façade of the house. The combination of entryway and second-floor window are intended to impress and draw attention to the house in a way that a simple doorway could not. The local artisans who built Jacob Ford Jr.'s house probably worked off regionally adapted designs utilizing regional materials.[45]

Besides the entryway and second-floor window, the rest of the façade is restrained. The white painted flush board siding on the front is contrasted with beaded clapboard on the sides and back. The main house has twelve-over-twelve sash windows, while the kitchen wing has six-over-six.[46] The wood-frame house is built on a rubble granite masonry foundation. The wood shingle hip roof of the main house "is capped with a small gable roof running between the brick chimneys."[47] The house without the Palladian entryway combination could be mistaken for simply an overgrown farmhouse on first glance given the relative lack of architectural embellishments.[48] The Ford mansion undoubtedly drew attention among the local residents when it was constructed. And it no doubt immediately drew attention once the war started as a place in which to quarter troops and to establish a headquarters several years later in 1779, when the Continental army camped for the winter in Morristown.[49]

The mansion drew attention not only for its size, but also for its location and the way the architecture took advantage of the natural setting. This blending was described in 1938 by a National Park Service architect. He wrote:

> [T]*he design of the house…is characterized by simplicity and repose, with the emphasis placed on horizontals. The strong lines of the base, belt course and cornice are in harmony with the window treatment where equal tiers of windows, upstairs and down, with their shutters, continue the horizontal character. These elements and the fine hipped roof with its widely splayed eaves combine to make the house fit the site on top of the slope in a very successful way.*[50]

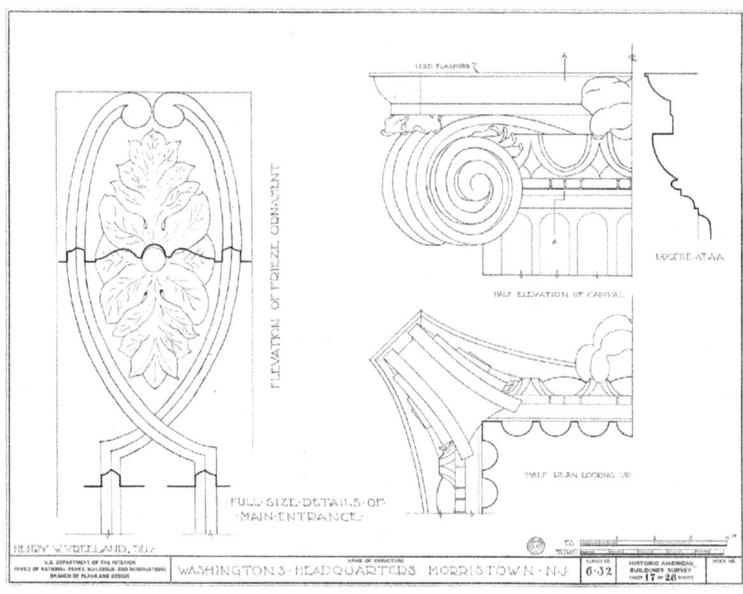

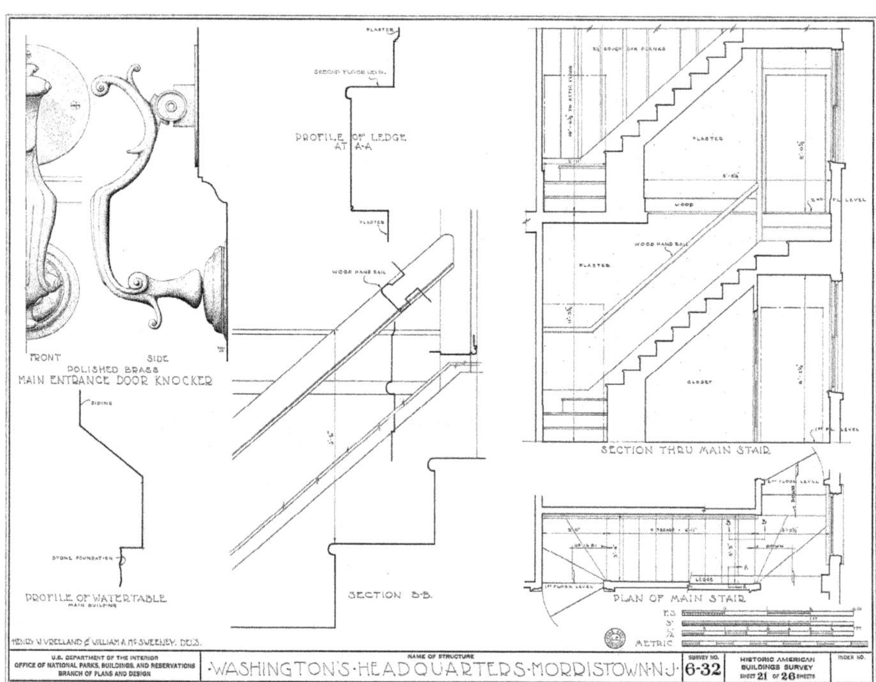

Top: Measured drawing of an architectural detail of the front entrance of the Ford Mansion, 1939. *Historic American Buildings Survey.*

Bottom: Measured detail of original stairway and front door knocker of the Ford Mansion, 1939. *Historic American Buildings Survey.*

Detail showing flush boards on south side of the mansion with a portion of dentil molding, 1939. *Historic American Buildings Survey.*

Upon entering the mansion, the parlor presents another contrast. In most mansions, "The preeminence of the formal parlor in house plans of the period confirms the ruling ideas of mansions."[51] While the Fords had a grand parlor space-wise, it was as similarly plain in decorative appointments as the rest of the house. The walls are plaster with a simple wood-panel dado and chair rail.

On many architectural levels, the Ford Mansion is a contradiction. The exterior embellishments and the size of the house clearly mark it as a mansion for the genteel society. The presence of a parlor and a grand hall on the interior also mark the Ford house as a mansion.[52] The hidden stairway and the lack of interior ornamentation tend to show the house, though, in more of a simple flavor. The lack of a broad monumental stairway in the Ford Mansion also has a practical answer. While "[s]tairs signified an ascent to grand rooms where guest were received with proper dignity,"[53] the Fords may never have intended to entertain on such a scale and therefore had no need for guests to ascend to the second floor. Having the stairs tucked away to one side, out of sight of the main hall, left the first-floor and the second-floor hall completely open for entertaining or other large gatherings.

The absence of ornamental qualities at the Ford Mansion can conceivably stem from many causes. Perhaps the Fords felt that they had spent enough on the structure; perhaps they overspent; perhaps local craftsmen were unable to fashion some of the decorative elements; or perhaps their religious sensibilities were at their limits. Naturally, without documentation from the Fords themselves, inference based on similar projects is the best substitute for determining the Fords' motivation and desires.

How this mansion fit in with the social aspirations of the Fords is unknown. The Ford family was already quite prominent and well known by 1772. Not only did they enjoy the privilege of voting due to their financial status, but they were also the individuals being elected to office. Only through inference are we able to surmise that they intended the house to be a showpiece, as did virtually anyone building on such a scale.[54] The inference about the Fords' motivation can be ascertained in part by consolidating the desires of their peers who left more complete records.

It was by far the largest home in Morristown, and Morris County, and would be for many years to come.[55] To understand the role the house played, "[W]e must look more closely at the [mansion itself] and locate [it] within the matrix of other houses in the village."[56] In neighboring Delaware, 90 percent of the houses built between 1760 and 1830 were six hundred square feet or less, and the figures are comparable for New Jersey. The Ford Mansion is nine thousand square feet.

Perhaps the Fords simply had more money than social ambition or architectural finesse. It seems unlikely that a homeowner would build a mansion like this one to be inconspicuous. The main purpose of such grand houses "was to convey the gentility of the owner, to act as a sort of billboard of his accomplishments."[57] To understand why the mansion was built, it is necessary to look at the societal structure that produced residents of considerable wealth. What roles these individuals played within their respective societies will help to explain the existence of the mansion and its role during the Revolution.

OUTSIDE THE MANSION

Eighteenth-century mansions were in many respects considered incomplete without a formal garden to enhance the landscape and the approach to the structure. "A garden, including the front courtyard, created an artificially refined space from which the house itself could rise to greet its visitor."[58] The gardens provided outdoor space that paralleled the indoor space in grandeur. The overall effect would be a seamless flow, an uninterrupted parade of the owner's wealth and taste.

There is no evidence that the Ford family had any type of formal, or even informal, decorative garden near the mansion to lend embellishment to the landscape. Concerning the mansion, "Explicit landscape documentation and extant above ground features are relatively absent."[59] As with certain architectural features not being represented physically in the mansion, certain features are also lacking of traditional eighteenth-century mansion garden design, which creates more questions than it answers. As with the architectural features, many possible reasons for why the Ford family excluded formal gardens exist, too.[60]

As no evidence of formal gardens has been found, it is safe to conclude that the "property included pastureland for grazing horses and other domestic animals, perhaps a kitchen garden, and many outbuildings."[61] This understanding lends more strength to the belief that the mansion was not necessarily intended as the seat of a business tycoon. Rather it was more likely that it was to be the focus of a large working farm of a family of considerable means.

Mr. Corbit

By way of a brief comparison to Jacob Ford Jr., William Corbit began to build a comparably grand Georgian mansion about one hundred miles south of Morristown in Odessa, Delaware, in 1772. Corbit certainly faced many of the main concerns that Ford faced concerning the troubled relations with Great Britain. While Corbit shared concern, he did not share Ford's patriotic impulses. Though not a Loyalist, William Corbit was neutral in his approach to politics. As a Quaker, he theoretically opposed armed conflict.

Corbit's mansion, however, differs from Ford's in three significant ways. The Corbit Mansion exterior is brick, whereas the Ford Mansion is painted flush board (front façade) and clapboards; the Corbit Mansion has elegantly appointed interior embellishments, while the Ford Mansion does not, at least not to the extent the Corbit Mansion does; and finally, the Corbit Mansion has a broad open stairway, whereas the Ford Mansion has a small, concealed stairway. Further, Corbit's mansion was built by master craftsmen who could utilize a pattern book such as Abraham Swan's *The British Architect* or *Designs in Architecture*. The detail work was of the finest to be found anywhere in the colony.

Perhaps the most significant difference for historians between the two is the level of documentation. "The Corbit House is one of the best-documented houses in America," according to John Sweeney.[62] Dates, monetary expenses and names of some of the builders are known through the extensive diaries, letters and other manuscripts. Corbit was a tanner and farmer whose business is nearly as well documented. Visitors often left accounts of the fabulous

The William Corbit Mansion in Odessa, Delaware.

mansion in their writings, which are detailed and describe the estate, unlike the Ford Mansion, which has no known references. Corbit also lived in his mansion for nearly forty years, unlike Ford Jr., who died during the war. The main comparison and difference is really what we can determine and "know" about how the two men and their families lived and utilized their estates—and, further, how the societies in which they lived responded and what expectations they had of the men who commanded such resources.

While all of these differences are architecturally important, they do not exclude one house or the other from the rarified realm of "mansion." The first impression of the Corbit Mansion leaves an impact, which overwhelms as compared with the Ford Mansion.

Cultural Considerations

Even though this colonial mansion of Jacob Ford Jr. lacks certain refining elements architecturally, it does have all the hallmarks of a home of someone who seemingly was not anticipating going to war with England in the near future. Yet, oddly, overall this difficult and uncertain period was noted as a time experiencing a "new wave of mansion building."[63] It seems quite possible that a colonial homeowner would most likely have not been too involved with the disputes raging in the colonies to distract from the building of a structure on the scale of the Ford Mansion. Men of wealth and status are not generally seen as advocating political and economic upheaval. Yet, a man of wealth would no doubt have been looked to for advice on the deteriorating conditions. But would it not seem reasonable to stay above the fray to the extent it would otherwise jeopardize or keep him from pursuing his interests? Jacob Ford Jr. chose, for reasons not completely known, to enter the fray rather than to stay above it. Ford Jr., in fact, became so involved that he did neglect certain finishing touches on his family's mansion due to his increased activity in colonial causes.[64] The upper floors of the mansion were not even whitewashed until Washington arrived. Simultaneously, with construction, Ford Jr. became more involved with the radical politics of opposing British policy.

The political, legal, social and economic aspirations of the colonists were quickly evolving into new approaches to how one would, or should, live their life. The possibilities multiplied as each year passed during the 1770s. In 1772, though, the horrors of war were as yet unspoken, and the glory promised through a military career still beckoned. The world in which the Fords created their mansion was one where the past still held a tremendous sway over the future. In New Jersey, situated between New York and Philadelphia, the tides of impending revolution had yet to reach the high landing ascending to the magnificent entryway at the Ford mansion. Jacob Ford Jr. naturally was aware of the problems that the colonies faced. With his family iron business, Ford would have been seen as an independent man familiar with risk and reward. The Ford mansion, and others like it, represented a society and system that was too stable, too secure and too rigid to suggest political turmoil. Yet turmoil was raging all throughout New Jersey. Colonial America was rapidly giving way to something quite unlike colonial America.[65] Whatever Ford Jr. may have felt in 1772, when construction began, it surely included a sense of resignation that events would ultimately work out in his favor. Building a mansion is too optimistic for second guesses.

Conclusions

Before leaving the Ford family in this chapter and moving to the Revolutionary years in the next chapter, it is worthwhile to reiterate that the family in 1775, the year armed conflict in the Revolution started, was well established in Morristown. Like many other ambitious and hardworking families, they had accomplished quite a lot since Morris County was established in 1739. From the beginning, the Fords were prominent civic leaders and successful businessmen.

Theodosia Ford, Jacob Ford Jr.'s widow, dominates the Revolutionary period of the Ford family history. Forced to accept a leadership role in the family after her husband and father-in-law's deaths, Mrs. Ford held the family together and kept the farm and family business a profitable endeavor. While, sadly, no correspondence of Mrs. Ford's survives (save one piece that will be discussed later and a few legal documents wherein she acts as a witness), we can again by inference determine some of the decisions she made based on the available evidence.

The two years after the deaths of Jacob Ford Jr. and Jacob Ford Sr., before Washington arrived, obviously must have been very difficult for Mrs. Ford. Widowed at thirty-eight, she was left with a mansion, over two hundred acres, a farm and orchard, a gunpowder mill and four children, the oldest of whom was a young teenager. While little or no direct information concerning her activities is known, it would seem odd that the surviving wife of such a prominent businessman and civic leader would suddenly cut off her ties to the community, particularly in the middle of a war that her husband played such a role in facilitating. In one way, she could now see herself as vulnerable to British or Loyalist attacks, which were pervasive during the war, particularly at the beginning. "The problem was acute because of the sheer numbers who opposed the struggle for independence."[66] Her true feelings on the cause, though, are wholly unknown. We only assume that she shared her husband's passion to oppose British policy to the point of armed conflict. So much of the Ford family private life remains a mystery. Whether this was due to

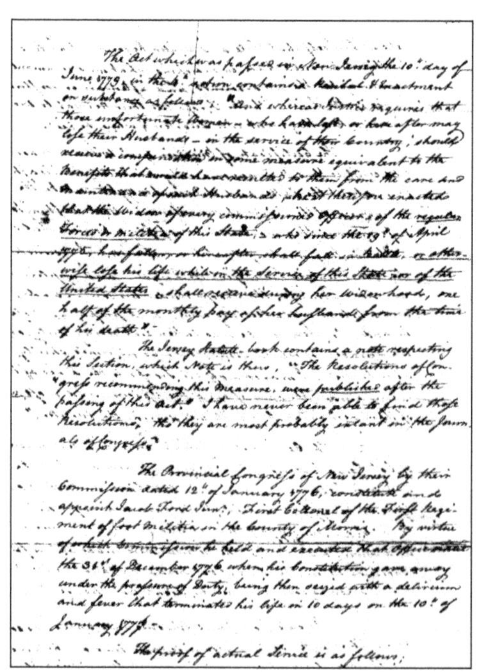

The Act which was passed in New Jersey the 10th day of June 1779, in the [illegible] section contains [illegible] & enactment or substance as follows: "And whereas Justice requires that those unfortunate Women who have lost or hereafter may lose their Husbands in the service of their Country, should receive a compensation in some measure equivalent to the benefits that would have resulted to them from the care and maintenance of such Husbands; Be it therefore enacted that the Widow of every commissioned Officer of the regular Forces or militia of this State, who since the 19th of April 1775, has fallen, or hereafter shall fall in battle, or otherwise lose his life while in the service of this State or of the United States, shall receive during her widowhood, one half of the monthly pay of her husband from the time of his death."

The Jersey Statute-book contains a note respecting this Section, which Note is thus, "The Resolutions of Congress recommending this Measure, were published after the passing of this Act." I have never been able to find those Resolutions, tho' they are most probably extant in the Journals of Congress.

The Provincial Congress of New Jersey by their Commission dated 12th of January 1776, constituted and appointed Jacob Ford Junr., First Colonel of the First Regiment of foot Militia in the County of Morris. By virtue of which Commission he held and executed that Office until the 31st of December 1776 when his Constitution gave away under the pressure of Duty, being then seized with a delirium and fever that terminated his life in 10 days on the 10th of January 1777.

The proof of actual Service is as follows:

Account of the death of Colonel Jacob Ford Jr., 1777. *Morristown National Historical Park.*

intentional wishes or to unintentional circumstances is unknown.[67] The Ford Family Papers in the Morristown National Historical Park archives contain mainly business-related material.

As an independent woman, she was not alone in her newly found role. Many women whose husbands perished as a result of the war faced similar circumstances. Some succeeded; some did not. Some left their farms and businesses and moved on. Some no doubt moved to England. Many, though, faced the crushing prospect of having to provide for a young family while at the same time running the farm or family business or both. Few women were as fortunate as Theodosia Ford in being left with a substantial financial reservoir from which to draw. Sadly, without any record maintained by Mrs. Ford, it is hard to decipher what actually happened. It can only be surmised that she prospered as much as could be expected. She still owned the mansion—as guardian for her children—when Washington arrived in 1779, and the farm and family business were seemingly operating as well. When Washington arrived, Mrs. Ford was only forty years old.

Women in New Jersey generally fared better than their sisters in other states. New Jersey was the only state constitution created during the Revolution, which allowed women the right to vote. This progressive view toward women may have benefited Mrs. Ford during the war. The right to vote was short-lived though, as it was rescinded in 1807.[68]

The eldest son, Timothy, named for his maternal grandfather the minister, was born on December 4, 1762. After the death of his father Jacob Ford Jr. in 1777, Timothy anxiously took on the role of soldier.[69] He served at several locations after his sixteenth birthday and was wounded at Springfield, New Jersey. Oddly, Springfield was the same location where his father Ford Jr. led the Morris County militia in December 1776, one month before dying of pneumonia. Timothy later graduated from Princeton and was admitted to the bar in New York.

Timothy moved with his sister Elizabeth and her husband, Henry William De Saussure, to Charleston, South Carolina, in 1785. Timothy Ford records in his diary for October 1, 1785, of the tearful departure from Morristown. "My dear Mother parted with her only daughter as tho' for the last time. It was a scene of tears indeed."[70] He soon married and took up the practice of law in Charleston. His first wife, Sarah Amelia De Saussure, was actually his sister's sister-in-law. He quickly became a prominent member in civic life and served in the South Carolina legislature. He died on December 7, 1830.

Theodosia Ford saith she is the widow of Col. Jacob Ford Junr. deceased, who died the day of January 1777, leaving by her five children, to wit, Timothy, born December 1763; Gabriel, born Janry 9 1765; Elizabeth born and married afterward to Henry Wm. DeSaussure; Jacob, born & Phebe born who died under four years old: That the provision in her husband's will in lieu of her Dower she accepted as ~~such~~ [illegible] That she remembers to have heard of the sale of some of her husband's forges and rough lands after his death to John Jacob Faesch; but never understood that Moses Tuttle had any part of the said land or was to pay the estate for it ~~[illegible]~~ until within one or two years past: nor any conversation like it among any of her ~~children~~ surviving children though they continued members of her family always till they married or went into business, excepting absences at College & for the purposes of [illegible] education. She also says that ~~Col. Jacob Ford~~ [illegible] the father of her husband died in about a week after his said son: That the Revd. Timothy Johnes her father ~~was~~ minister of the Gospel was settled at Morristown, and according to the best of her belief she thinks his knowledge of Iron works and rough mountain lands about Mount Pleasant, the Middle forge, and Burnt meadow, and the values thereof was exceedingly limited and vague: that Moses Tuttle has been the owner or conductor of iron works at Mount-Pleasant or near that place ever since she can remember him there which is ago, and how much longer she cannot tell: that he was always esteemed by her husband and she thinks by most of other people for his understanding & good [illegible]

Summary of facts in the case of *Ford v. Tuttle. Morristown National Historical Park.*

Gabriel Ford, the second eldest child, acquired full ownership of the mansion from his brothers and sister in 1805. It is from Gabriel that the most extensive writings about the house are known to exist. Even this amount of material from Gabriel is slight. Yet, it is all that is known to enable us to catch a glimpse of the Ford family firsthand in the nineteenth century. Secondly, the glimpse from Gabriel Ford offers invaluable insight into how the mansion was maintained and modernized during the first half of the nineteenth century. "In general…[the] entries are interesting in their specificity, and illuminate some first third of the 19th century building practices and prices."[71]

The entries in Gabriel's journals begin about 1814 with undated entries and end in October 1837. Over the course of twenty-three years, he kept a record of what he thought the most memorable aspects in the mansion's life. The first entry, undated, mentions six previous dates :

1774	*The house was built by Col. Jacob Ford, Jr.*
1793	*Lombardy poplars were planted before the door.*
1796	*Lombardy poplars were planted along the road.*
1797	*Lombardy poplars were planted by the drawing room window.*
	Ronsilet Pear was planted in the backyard.
1796	*Stable had new sills, roof and enclosure.*
1797	*Barn was raised up with new sills.*[72]

This seems a strange list of events to compile. It could be that so little had changed with the mansion since Gabriel acquired the estate outright that not much was worth reporting.

One interesting entry that affects the mystery of whether a door existed on the west wall of Washington's office was recorded on August 11, 1820. Gabriel writes, "Porches to the front and office doors and steps to the back door [?] made and painted."[73] Only circumstantial evidence exists to indicate exactly how George Washington utilized the mansion and what changes he may have made.

Further discussion of the nineteenth-century Ford family will resume in the next chapter. There are distinct phases in the life of the mansion in relation to the family. It is unique that the family had possession of the mansion for nearly one hundred years. While this is not unheard of, it is unusual, particularly given the situation in which Mrs. Ford found herself after the death of her husband and father-in-law in the same month.

With few legal rights, Mrs. Ford was able to keep her family together and keep her family's property together. Certainly the reputations of her husband

and father-in-law in the community helped her. But there can be no doubt that Mrs. Ford faced a challenge that few colonial women did. While many lost their husbands, few were thrust into a leadership role beyond the family like Mrs. Ford. She had to maintain the family business, the source of the wealth the family enjoyed and the legacy of her husband and father-in-law. In many respects in terms of the mansion, the real hero, the real patriot, is Theodosia Ford.

CHAPTER 3

The American Revolution and the Mansion as Headquarters

A Brief Background

By the time of the arrival of armed conflict with Great Britain in 1775, New Jersey had already experienced its own internal episodes of conflict. Much of this was due to the land distribution practices of the New Jersey Proprietors.[74]

In the 1740s, the Colony of New Jersey experienced violent tenant riots. In 1735, a land survey found that in Hunterdon County alone over one hundred families occupied over thirteen thousand acres collectively without one title among them.[75] At the first signs of trouble, the East and West New Jersey Proprietors, being the large landowners by virtue of being descended from the royal patent of 1664, decided to try their arguments in court. East New Jersey Proprietors particularly wanted to put an end to squatters. Unfortunately, violent altercations followed. For over ten years, the action simmered between the squatters, the proprietors, the courts and the governor. The situation reached a crisis point in 1749 when the threat of the introduction of royal troops finally eased the tensions.[76] New Jersey was not alone in land disputes.

Throughout the 1750s and 1760s, riots in the nearby Hudson Valley were frequently enflamed and would always simmer just below the surface.[77] In many of these cases, American landowners, as part of the local power structure in the colony, kept the poorer farmers at bay. The farmers would therefore look to Britain for help in an attempt to play two power brokers against one another. This distrust of the local farming interests for colonial

June 14, 1775

Gentlemen — Morris Town June 14th 1775

I am very sorry for the late Riots and disturbance which hath happened at the [illegible] Pond Mine, and hope it will be in the power of the Magistracy to interfere and prevent the like in future. Lord Stirlings conduct in seizing my property by Violence must surprize [illegible] when he knows me to have a good right to a great part of the Mine, [illegible] worked at the same [illegible] for a [illegible] Years [illegible] that the [illegible] he hath attempted to move was [illegible] my Expence, or at the Expence of Mr Erskine under me, [illegible] to Justify the taking of [illegible] by Violence and [illegible] circumstances I know not. [illegible] methods are taken to prevent him from doing the like in future, and for the preservation of the Peace, great Mischiefs will ensue. [illegible]

Discussion of the violence in and around Morristown, circa 1775. *Morristown National Historical Park.*

landowners would have to be overcome during the Revolution if success was to be achieved.

It is known that the 1760s were a time of tremendous economic crisis, with credit extremely tight and courts jammed with debt cases. The Currency Act of 1764 had prohibited New Jersey and other colonies from issuing paper currency, thus tightening the supply and putting cash only into the hands of the wealthy.[78] These conditions should not be overlooked in seeking to determine the motivation for those who chose to oppose Britain and those who chose to remain loyal to the Crown.

For East Jersey—there was a distinct difference in the way the two Jerseys experienced the Revolutionary War—the first semblance of organized opposition to British policy occurred early in 1766. The New York Sons of Liberty sought to expand its influence and sent letters to many of the communities within a fifty-mile radius in an attempt to strengthen resolve against the Stamp Act.[79]

Given the rising provincial tensions over credit and debt that were already in place before the British measures magnified the problem, the Sons of Liberty of New York had only limited success. "The revolutionary movement in East Jersey, in its formative period, was neither a response to local grievances nor simply the reaction to events in other colonies. It was a mutually reinforcing, generalized anxiety and rebellion over both imperial and provincial abuses."[80] The Jersey Sons of Liberty were more rhetorical than physical. "Public protest rather than extremist acts marked the protest movement in New Jersey."[81]

Prelude to War

The arrival of open warfare with Great Britain in Morristown was greeted much like it was in other segments of the colonies. The unique aspect for New Jersey in terms of participation, though, was its location. Lying between two of the most important cities in North America ensured that one side or another would continually be moving through some part of New Jersey.

A 1765 history of the Colony of New Jersey by Samuel Smith noted:

> *As the province has very little foreign trade on bottoms of its own, the produce of all kinds for sale, goes chiefly to New York and Philadelphia; much of it is there purchased for markets abroad, but some consumed among themselves.*[82]

Smith also lamented that "a century should pass, and very little appear abroad of what the settlers here have been doing, is not so much to be wondered at, when their difficulties in procuring a living are considerable."[83] The sense of abandonment, or of being ignored and seen for nothing more than a transit way, was magnified during the upcoming years of the Revolution.

After the war began in 1775, New Jersey quickly became involved in the strategic planning for both sides. The location of New Jersey was simply too important to be overlooked by either side. As has been commented on, New Jersey was a crossroads for both sides in the conflict, which ultimately created conflicting allegiances. Location is crucial in most wars or conflicts, and the Revolution was no exception. The first winter encampment at Morristown occurred in 1777 following the surprise American victories at Trenton and Princeton. "The Army arrived in Morristown on January 6, 1777 and occupied many farmhouses, houses, and other buildings in or near the village and from Princeton to Hudson Highlands."[84] It was at the beginning of this encampment that both Jacob Ford Sr. and Jacob Ford Jr. died. At the Ford Mansion were thirty-five Delaware troops who witnessed the deaths of both Jacob Ford Sr. and Jacob Ford Jr. The second winter encampment in 1779–80 to involve the Ford Mansion during the Revolution was the one to which much of the subsequent history of the property has generally looked for validation.

"By living in the major theater of war, Jerseymen suffered measurably more than most Americans, physically, materially, and psychologically."[85] Further, "Perhaps no other region was affected by the internal and external convulsions for as long or with such intensity."[86] In a letter to Aaron Burr in 1779, William Paterson wrote, "We are continually broke in upon by the Sons of Tumult and War, Our situation is such that the one Army or the other is almost constantly with us."[87] It was this location-related aspect that kept the war more apparent for a longer period of time as British troops were stationed in Manhattan until 1783, the year that the Treaty of Paris formally ended hostilities. This luck of location made allegiance much more imperative for those colonists who truly did not understand the magnitude of the conflict. While the cries of "liberty" or "no taxation" provided the eighteenth-century equivalent of a sound bite, few could knowledgably explain the root causes of the conflict and fewer still felt they had much at stake to actively pitch their support fully one way or the other.

The Ford family, given their wealth and social status, would reasonably be expected to have been circumspect in their approach to the conflict. Yet it was their status as community leaders that in part drove them to the colonial cause. The roots they had in New Jersey were deep, and at least three generations were actively involved in the affairs of their community. Furthermore, the financial investment made by the family over several decades was not to be lightly dismissed. "The men who first joined the Colonial militia were generally 'hallmarks of respectability or at least of full citizenship in their communities.'"[88]

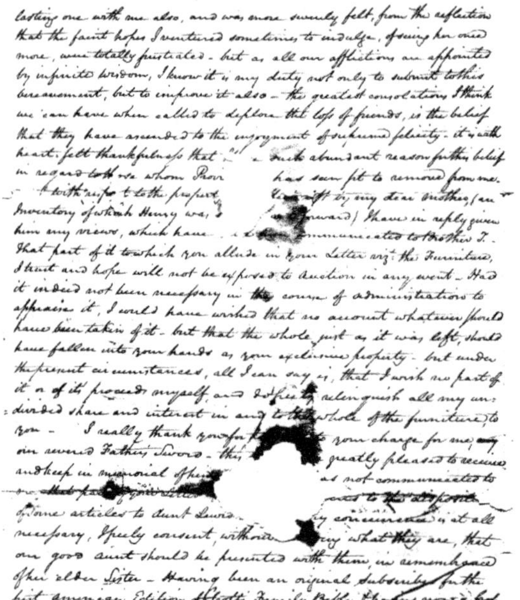

lasting one with me also, and was more severely felt, from the reflection that the faint hopes I ventured sometimes to indulge, of seeing her once more, were totally frustrated - but as all our afflictions are appointed by infinite wisdom, I know it is my duty not only to submit to this bereavement, but to improve it also - the greatest consolation I think we can have when called to deplore the loss of friends, is the belief that they have ascended to the enjoyment of supreme felicity - it is with heart-felt thankfulness that [illegible] such abundant reason for the belief in regard to those whom Prov[illegible] has seen fit to remove from me. - With respect to the property [illegible] left by my dear Mother, (an Inventory of which Henry was [illegible] forward) I have in reply given him my views, which have [illegible] communicated to brother T. - That part of it to which you allude in your Letter viz.t the Furniture, I trust and hope will not be exposed to Auction in any event - Had it indeed not been necessary in the course of administration to appraise it, I would have wished that no account whatever should have been taken of it - but that the whole, just as it was left, should have fallen into your hands as your exclusive property - but under the present circumstances, all I can say is, that I wish no part of it or of its proceeds myself, and do freely relinquish all my undivided share and interest in any to the whole of the furniture, to you - I really thank you for [illegible] your charge for me, our revered Father's Sword - this [illegible] greatly pleased to receive and keep in memorial of him [illegible] as not communicated to [illegible] of some articles to Aunt Lewis [illegible] is at all necessary, I freely consent, without [illegible] what they are, that our good aunt should be presented with them, in remembrance of her elder Sister - Having been an original Subscriber for the first American Edition of Scott's Family Bible & having now a copy, I am not in want of the set you mention - [illegible] as a favor,

Letter from Jacob Ford III to his brother, Gabriel, mentioning their father's sword. *Morristown National Historical Park.*

It is not surprising, then, that the family apparently had little hesitation even before the actual outbreak of armed hostilities. Before the mansion was completely finished, Jacob Ford Jr. had signed an agreement with the provincial legislature (of which he was a member) to manufacture gunpowder for the colony, and this agreement apparently remained in effect through the duration of the war. "Ford Jr. contracted with the Provincial Congress of New Jersey to erect a powder mill, and Congress agreed to pay him 2000 pounds of public money for one year without interest to be repaid in good merchantable powder."[89]

Local Considerations

The events of the early 1770s with respect to the political turmoil with Britain unfolded with a rapidity that is hard to imagine. In an age without electronic communication, news of events traveled at lightning speed for the era. The passions of colonists were fueled by reports that many times were a mixture of truth and falsehood. The motivations for opposition or support of any given piece of information were probably as varied as the people themselves. To ascribe one overarching sentiment to the colonists is an approach to the study of the Revolution that neglects the significant opposition to independence. In fact, the Revolution in many ways succeeded in spite of itself given the fragmentary nature of the resistance to the British, particularly in a colony as diverse as New Jersey. In many ways, the "American Revolution was a product of thirteen individual rebellions as well as a general revolt against British authority."[90] In terms of New Jersey itself, it was a colony that did not exude the qualities associated with rebellion. "Though prosperous and stable, it was a small, dependent province."[91] One exhaustive study found that

> *Loyalists in New Jersey drew most of its adherents from the ranks of the common man and cut across class, economic, ethnic, and religious lines…the republican regime had more difficulty than its counterpart in any other state except…New York in suppressing royalists and establishing law and order.*[92]

The last of the British acts directed at the colonies before the conflict progressed to open rebellion were the aptly named the Intolerable Acts. In June 1774, the same year the Jacob Ford Jr. Mansion was finished enough to live in, Ford Jr. attended a meeting at the courthouse on the Green in Morristown. This meeting resolved to condemn "British taxation and the Intolerable Acts."[93] The meeting also determined that a convention of counties should meet, and they formed a committee of correspondence to handle their resolutions.[94]

The passage of the Intolerable Acts in 1774 must have been of great concern to the Fords, given the status of their new mansion. Until this time, Morristown was relatively free of mob reaction to local events of governmental abuse that was occurring around it in neighboring towns. Jacob Ford Jr. was certainly keenly aware of the issues and of the potential impact, given the history for explosive class conflict in the colony. Ford Jr. more than likely surveyed the situation and made a decision relatively early to support a more confrontational colonial response.

One possible reason, given the deep involvement both of Jacob Ford Sr. and Jacob Ford Jr. had in provincial government matters, was the Administration of Justice Act of 1774, which sought to suppress township government in Massachusetts. While aimed at Massachusetts, it certainly put other colonies on alert.[95] And given that both Jacob Ford Jr. and Jacob Ford Sr. were justices and heavily involved in colonial governmental activities, this was virtually an unthinkable provocation. Jacob Ford Jr. was also the high sheriff for Morris County. The colonies were essentially self-governing in their viewpoint, and much of their authority came from the courts. Jacob Ford Sr. first became a justice of the peace for Morris County in 1740, right after the inception of Morris County government. Jacob Ford Sr. would eventually serve over thirty years in this post, one of the longest on record, and during that time he clearly exercised considerable power.[96] The position of justice would have put Ford Sr. in a position of judicial authority, but also in a role as a local leader. His role nicely complemented his business interests, too, as the court often met in the early years in his tavern in Morristown.

Local judicial control was the foundation of colonial governments. The power to pass judgment implied the legal authority to determine the patterns and course of social interaction among citizens. The First Continental Congress adopted a resolution that enshrined this belief in the power of the local government. The American people had "a free and exclusive power of legislation in their provincial legislations, where there rights of legislation could alone be preserved in all cases of taxation and internal polity."[97] With this power removed, local governments were no longer seen as the arbiters of legal authority. Therefore, the passage of the Administration of Justice Act had a tremendous impact on the way colonials viewed and operated as citizens. It is no wonder that the Fords, who participated so actively in the administration of justice, would be so taken aback by the passage of an act designed to eliminate their power—and by extension the power of local government.

In May 1775, Morris County called a meeting of freeholders and residents for the purpose of organizing soldiers and funding for defense. Shortly

and assignes forever
have hereunto Set our hands and Seales this
Seventh Day of February in the year of
our Lord one Thousand Seven hundred and Seventy
Four
Seled and Delivered
in the presents of
Jacob Ford Junr
Stephen harriman

Meriam her X mark Harriman
Joseph Harriman

Whereof he the said Jacob Ford Senr Hath Thereunto interch
=angably Set his Hand and Seal the Day and year above
written
Sealed and Delivered
in the presence of
~~Andrew Whitehead~~
David Ford

Jacob Ford

Top: Signature of Jacob Ford Jr. as witness, 1774. *Morristown National Historical Park.*

Bottom: Signature of Jacob Ford Sr. as witness, circa 1775. *Morristown National Historical Park.*

after Morris County was formed in 1739, several of the most influential residents signed a petition to form a county militia. In their pledge of service, prompted partly by the war between Great Britain and Spain at the time, the militiamen swore allegiance to George II. When this petition was signed in 1742, among the prominent names was Jacob Ford Sr.[98] The Morris County militia did participate in holding back Indian uprisings in Pennsylvania and fought sporadically during the French and Indian War, although they were apparently never called upon to display their allegiance to the king in this conflict as in the early militia days. The county therefore had few veterans and a less-than-professional fighting force by the time the war arrived. Other nearby counties also had militias in place, with varying degrees of professionalism.

The Provincial Congress levied a £10,000 tax for the raising and equipping of a militia for the state. This act of the Provincial Congress was one of the first moves toward independence. On August 2, 1775, the Congress notified the General Assembly that it would now be the legislative body for New Jersey.[99] The next step in defense preparation occurred in August 1775 when New Jersey passed the Militia Act, which was essentially a conscription law. The Provisional Congress worked with the Continental Congress to enlist the required number of troops as armed conflict became more a matter of when, not if.

CULTURAL ASPECTS OF THE CONFLICT

At its base, the war was a civil conflict generated over constitutional issues exacerbated by internal imperial policy.[100] How *colonial* were the colonists legally? They were not colonists in the sense of having been a defeated people. The vast majority were British. "As British subjects, [they] could not be taxed except 'by their own consent, given personally or by their representatives.'"[101] In terms of who actually made decisions, the Declaratory Act firmly stated the British position relative to the right of Parliament to legislate for the colonies. However, did that right to legislate include taxation? Parliamentary taxation was the constitutional challenge upon which all others hung.[102] Yet, by 1774, the New Brunswick (New Jersey) Convention stated that based on the British constitution "imposing taxes for the purpose of raising revenue in America is unconstitutional and oppressive."[103] To the average farmer or tradesman, this was probably too much to digest. Who was in charge? Who would make the decisions?

The genius of the Revolutionary leaders was to narrow these massive origins of conflict down to contained portions. The question became not who has the power, but who *should* have the power. The previous fifty years or so had taught the small landowner or farmer to be highly suspicious of the local ruling elite. And the local ruling elite needed to be very cautious in how it framed a struggle that could benefit them above all others. "The fact that the lower ranks were involved in the contest should not obscure the fact that the contest itself was generally a struggle for office and power between members of an upper class: the new against the established."[104] Some ethereal concept like "liberty" or "freedom" was precisely what the elite saw as their best option for enticing the lower classes to join in the movement. By relying on arguments that could be understood at a visceral level, the Revolutionary leaders found a method of condensing the complex constitutional issues to simple, digestible motives that, in part, helped to promote a soldier class to fight. This obviously was critical to the Patriot cause. Few soldiers would get motivated enough to fight based on a handful of constitutional issues that were for the most part incomprehensible. This strategy worked reasonably well throughout most of the colonies. New Jersey, however, as the transit point for troops, ideas and loyalties, found it difficult to accept just one approach to the psychological aspects of the war.

Both American and British forces looked to the East Jersey region with its abundant agricultural production to provision their armies. Unfortunately, many farmers were hesitant to sell to the American army due to the weakness of the colonial currency.[105] This is one of the further ironies of the entire war. Farmers and tradesmen seemed more willing to offer their personal services rather than supply the army with their wares. Conversely, the black market selling of commodities to the British was quite strong in East Jersey because the British paid in hard currency, which was not subject to constant devaluation. A system of extensive smuggling had slowly developed over the years in the wake of the passage of the Townshend Acts of 1767.[106] This network become nearly the standard business model in East New Jersey by the time of the Revolution and ultimately worked against the American forces.

New Jersey residents suffered greatly from destruction of property at the hands of both sides. Although the claims accumulated against the British totaled more in the end. New Jersey "ranked fourth in the number of individuals who filed official claims with the British government after the war for compensation for losses sustained in support of the King."[107] Strangely, during the encampments, Washington routinely would defend his troops against charges of theft and destruction publicly. Privately, Washington seemed quite fickle about how he chose to discipline his troops. Starvation caused soldiers to act in ways they otherwise would not. Obtaining food was a constant challenge. Many times Washington attempted to secure the collaboration of local officials to give a veneer of local authorization to his culinary impressments.

Revolutionary New Jersey was a complicated and dangerous place. However, "By the end of 1777 the military situation stabilized and the line between rebel and royalist became more distinct. Political positions solidified and emotions intensified during the next six years as New Jersey experienced the trauma of a vicious civil war."[108] The vicissitudes of war were never so fully exhibited as they were in New Jersey, although "few families divided their allegiance."[109] The colony is often claimed to represent a microcosm of the larger war effort. If this is indeed the case, the Revolution must surely be one of the most conflicted engagements in history to have actually succeeded. Overall, "General enthusiasm for the war was not strong."[110] John Adams had estimated that one third of the population supported the war, one third opposed the war and one third was indifferent.[111] It has similarly been estimated that only one third of New Jersey residents were ardent supporters of the war, as well.[112]

Furthermore, "Leaders on both sides in the American Revolution acknowledged the existence of a substantial number of persons in New Jersey who gave their loyalty neither to the rebels not to the king."[113] It is important to distinguish between neutrals and Loyalists. While Loyalists and Patriots clearly had their affiliations, neutrals were simply those who had no real interest in which side won. These figures indicating less than majority support for independence in New Jersey point further to the important role played by foreign powers in the victory of the overall Patriot cause, particularly the French.

HOW THE WAR PROGRESSED

In January 1775, after the First Continental Congress had met, the New Jersey Provisional Congress took up its grievance measures with Governor Franklin. A new county committee was formed, with Jacob Ford Jr. as a member, which was to attend meetings of the Provincial Congress. This county committee would ensure that information would be relayed to the residents and that residents had some voice in the Provincial Congress.

The meeting of the First Continental Congress seems to have moved the debate one step further to civil conflict within East Jersey. Perhaps due to the more defiant nature of the East Jersey territory, perhaps because all but one of New Jersey's representatives to the First Continental Congress came from the East, this half of New Jersey seemed more decisive in its move toward armed conflict. Even before the conflict, students at the College of New Jersey at Princeton engaged in property destruction when they imitated the Boston Tea Party and destroyed several pounds of British tea. At the same time, more vocal opposition to the colonial attempts to oppose British policy started to balance the voices being raised against Great Britain, too. There was no monolithic approach to British "tyranny."

Simultaneously, each township created a committee of observance to enforce the resolutions of the Continental Congress.[114] These committees were particularly fond of enforcing mandates on the willing and unwilling. People "grew weary of being bullied by local committees of safety, by corrupt deputy assistant commissaries of supply, and by bands of ragged strangers with guns in their hands calling themselves soldiers of the Revolution."[115] The irony, of course, is that while the committee found the actions of the British Parliament to be in violation of their civil liberties, it apparently found nothing wrong with engaging in the violation of New Jerseyans' own civil liberties.

In the annals of the war in New Jersey, the Council of Safety, which operated from 1777 to 1778, was particularly offensive. This "thirteen man board, presided over by the Governor, had nearly absolute control over the lives and fortunes of Dissenters."[116] There are no accurate numbers on how many dissenters were affected by this and other similar groups.

This hatred continued long after the war ended in 1783, too. "Vigilante groups were formed to ensure that former enemies would be excluded from meaningful participation in the political order."[117] The most outrageous obstruction of justice occurred after the war, though, when "the legislature, in direct violation of the Treaty of Paris...failed to provide restitution of property of Loyalists."[118] This was a tactic not limited to New Jersey. Many of the new states found it difficult to enforce all the measures of the Treaty of Paris, particularly those affecting restitutions to British businesses and individuals. This obvious breach of one of the United States' first international treaties continued throughout the 1780s and was one of the issues prompting the creation of the Constitution. After the Constitution, the issue figured prominently in several early Supreme Court cases.

Washington at the Ford Mansion

Washington is often referred to as having picked Morristown due to the defensive nature of its topography. While this is true in part, Morristown also provided easy access to abundant steel-making, slitting mills and iron mine activities. These industries provided "ammunition and iron implements" in great numbers to the army.[119] Among the many types of iron items necessary to the army were "chains, bridle-bits, curry-combs, pots, kettles, canteens, hammers, shovels, axes, screws, horseshoes, anvils, wagon tires, and stove plates."[120] Materials of this nature were naturally as important to an army

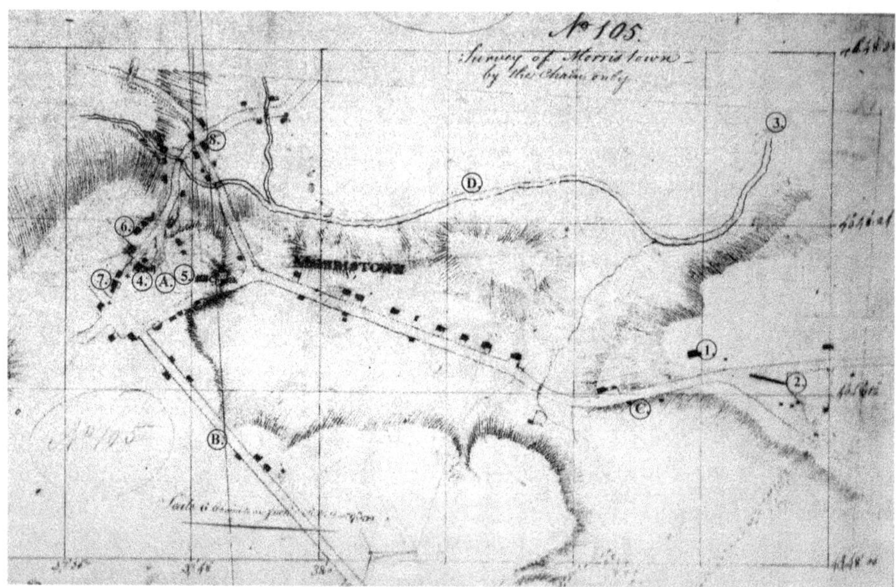

Early survey of Morristown, circa 1775. Number 1 is the Ford Mansion. *Morristown National Historical Park.*

as to a system of defense. New Jersey therefore proved too advantageous for Washington in 1779 for a variety of reasons, not just one.

George Washington arrived at the Ford Mansion early in December 1779. There are many reasons why Washington chose the mansion for his headquarters during his second stay in Morristown. Mrs. Ford apparently offered her home for his use, although the exact sequence of events between Washington and Mrs. Ford is unknown. In its favor, the mansion was the largest home in town, it was well known among the locals and it was located at the intersection of two major roads in New Jersey. Also, by choosing the mansion, Washington no doubt intended a long encampment and wanted to make sure that he and Mrs. Washington would have a comfortable stay. Washington was aware from the 1777 encampment that Morristown offered a good selection of natural resources (timber, produce and water) with which to sustain a large, ten-thousand-man army in Jockey Hollow for an extended period. Again, location played a crucial role in Morristown as it was located near the American capital in Philadelphia and also to the British in Manhattan. This proximity allowed Washington to keep surveillance on the British. Morristown was also situated so that forests, swamps and mountains surrounded it, making for a natural defensive position. Morristown's natural barriers and relative remoteness also allowed "Washington to conceal his low numbers of troops, as well as their miserable condition, from the British."[121]

Nature conspired against the army during 1779–80. One of the driest summers on record produced a greatly diminished harvest and caused rivers and streams to run very low, thus preventing the grinding of what grains were available. The winter of 1779–80 was the most difficult of the war from the standpoint of the weather. Morristown's enormous snowfall in 1779–80, ferocious winds and bitter cold made the Valley Forge encampment seem almost tame by comparison. Naturally, that is hyperbole, but Morristown was more severe than Valley Forge in terms of weather. Washington had to be constantly on guard for mutiny, and the weather only magnified his fear.

As with other winter encampments during the war, Washington had to deal with the usual challenges of "weather, logistics, inflated currency, and morale."[122] These issues did not suddenly spring to the fore only during winter encampments, of course. Washington's struggle seemed never-ending, and the topics were all too familiar to Washington and to the Continental Congress. A survey of Washington's letters during this period show the range of topics with which he was occupied. Washington wrote

Kitchen hearth in the Ford Mansion, 1939. *Historic American Buildings Survey.*

South wall of Washington's office inside the Ford Mansion. Note the absence of the fireplace, circa 1920. *Morristown National Historical Park.*

West wall of Washington's office inside of the Ford Mansion, circa 1920. *Morristown National Historical Park.*

about, "alliances with France and Spain; movements and quartering of his troops in New York, Philadelphia and in the southern Colonies; the enlistments and reenlistments soldiers, and the recruitment prospects for the upcoming campaign; the promoting of officers...the sentences and punishments for soldiers...and, of course, the movements and predicted activities of British troops in New York City and upstate, in the south, and into New Jersey."[123]

During the nearly seven months that Washington was in residence at the Ford Mansion, two rooms (the southeast and the northeast on the first floor—along with kitchen privileges) were allocated for Mrs. Ford and her family. The rest of the mansion was given over to Washington as his military headquarters. It is known that Washington also built several outbuildings to relieve the burden on the overcrowded mansion.

In addition to Washington himself, the regular occupants over the winter included Mrs. Washington and Washington's aides Alexander Hamilton (future secretary of the treasury), Robert Harrison (future Supreme Court nominee), Tench Tilghman, Richard Meade and James McHenry. There were also eighteen servants, including slaves, which Washington had with him. There would also have been a constant stream of visitors and dignitaries present in the mansion. Across the street, Washington's lifeguard was camped. Needless to say, it was a very busy place. Sadly, even during the second encampment, the mansion again witnessed the death of a figure associated with the conflict. On a visit to Washington, Spanish minister to the Continental Congress Don Juan de Maralles took ill and died in the mansion. The occasion warranted a full military funeral.

Conclusions

The amount of written material related to the American Revolution is astronomical. Trying to quantify it in itself would be a full-time job. George Washington spent nearly seven months at the mansion, and to this date no record directly from Mrs. Ford is known to exist, with one exception.

On July 21, 1780, Theodosia Ford wrote a letter to Washington's headquarters in an effort to secure a certificate from Washington that could be redeemed for reimbursement for the use of her home during the 1779–80 winter encampment. In the letter, presumably in Mrs. Ford's hand, she states that "the commissioners sent by General Greene to this place in order to settle the charges brought against the public are arrived."[124] Mrs. Ford knew that reimbursement would not be paid unless those who have quartered in an individual home provided a certificate to the owner that could then be redeemed. Apparently, other Morristown residents had certificates for the use of their homes, and Mrs. Ford surmised that "the hurry and confusion with which the General left the house I humbly presume is the reason why I did not also receive one."[125] Mrs. Ford wrote to Richard Meade, one of Washington's aide-de-camps who stayed in the Ford Mansion and who was no doubt known by Mrs. Ford. She asked that a certificate be prepared and delivered to her "specifying the time, how long, and the number of rooms occupied by the family."[126]

Richard Meade responded immediately with a letter dated July 21, 1780, that included the certificate that read:

> *I certify that the Commander in Chief took up his quarter at Mrs. Fords at Morris Town the first day of December 1779, that he left them the 23rd of June 1780, and that he occupied two Rooms below; all the upper floor, Kitchen, Cellar and Stable. The Stable was built and the two Rooms above the Stairs finished at the public expence, and a well, which was intirely useless and filled up before, put in thorough repair by walling &c. Head Qrs. Near Passaick July 26th. 1780.*[127]

Without exaggeration, these two pieces of correspondence are the most important manuscripts for establishing the intrinsic historical significance of the mansion during the Revolution. Mrs. Ford, whatever her patriotic motivations, clearly wanted some remuneration for the time her home was transformed into a military headquarters. With just this one piece of information, again, presumably from her hand, she seems to be no less distant from us now than if this document had not survived.

We know what we do about the time Washington spent by gleaning information from numerous sources that left glimpses of the seven months on which the subsequent history of the mansion rests. The Washington period represents only .0055 percent of the entire history of the mansion from the perspective of time, as of 2008. Based on that, it would seem that a disproportionate amount of time is spent on that story. If approached, however, from a historical standpoint, perhaps the Washington period is given a proper amount of time.

There are many fine studies of New Jersey during the Revolutionary War. It is not the purpose of this book to attempt a systematic review of the eight years of war during which the colony emerged as a state. The bibliography provides titles for further reading on specific topics.

Beginning with the next chapter, a different aspect in the history of the mansion will become the focus for the remainder of the book. Rather than the colonial and Revolutionary periods themselves, I will focus on the periods that look back at the colonial and Revolutionary periods for inspiration.

CHAPTER 4

The Mansion and the Family in Nineteenth-Century New Jersey

The War Is Over

Following the end of the Revolution, the mansion reverted back to being a home. The Ford family had lost three members during the war and emerged at the end of it, by all accounts, still in possession of the mansion, farm and iron business. Mrs. Ford had four children remaining, three sons and one daughter. Within five years of Washington's departure, her daughter Elizabeth married and moved to South Carolina. Her eldest son, Timothy, also moved to South Carolina with his sister and her husband. Gabriel, and his younger brother Jacob stayed in Morristown at the mansion with their mother.

Much of the history of the Ford family and the mansion after the Revolutionary War is dominated by the same forces that brought the family power and wealth before the war. Civic engagement by the Ford sons and a continuance of the iron and agricultural pursuits ensured that the family would remain prosperous and active in local affairs. It was mentioned previously that after Washington's departure in June 1780, Mrs. Ford must have kept the family, the mansion and the family business operating. While surviving records are inconclusive from Mrs. Ford to substantiate this, it is clear from inference. Her second-eldest son, Gabriel Ford, who would come to own the mansion and farm solely by 1805, spent his life partly managing the family's business interests in addition to his own legal career. Gabriel's work would not have been possible had his mother not maintained the family fortune in some form after her husband passed away.

Know all men by these presents that I Gabriel H. Ford of Morristown in the County of Morris & State of New Jersey am held and firmly bound unto Jacob Ford Esq.r of Charleston South Carolina in the sum of Six Thousand dollars, to be paid to the said Jacob or his certain Attorney, executors, administrators or assigns, and to the payment whereof I bind myself my heirs, executors and administrators firmly by these presents: sealed with my seal and dated the eighteenth day of April in the year of our Lord eighteen hundred and five — 1805.

The Condition of the above obligation is such that if the said Gabriel H. Ford his heirs, executors or administrators shall well and truly pay or cause to be paid unto the said Jacob Ford or his certain attorney, executors, administrators or assigns the just and full sum of Three thousand dollars, within five years from the date hereof, together with lawful Interest for the same from the first day of July in the year of our Lord eighteen hundred & six until paid & that without fraud or further delay. then the above obligation to be void otherwise to remain in full force and virtue.

Sealed & Delivered in the presence of —

Theodosia Ford
Anna Randolph

Gab. H. Ford

amo.t of above Bond — $3000.
Int. from 1st July 1806 to 1st July 1816 ; 10 Yrs @ $210 p ann. 2100.
$5100

Gabriel Ford's bond to his brother, Jacob, in Charleston, South Carolina, for $6,000. Notice the signature of Theodosia Ford as witness, April 1805. *Morristown National Historical Park.*

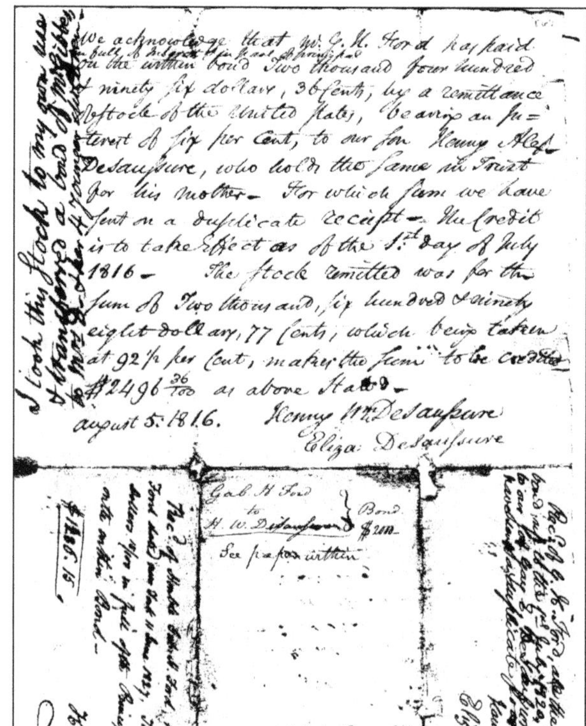

We acknowledge that Mr. G. H. Ford has paid on the within bond Two thousand four hundred & ninety six dollars, 36 cents, by a remittance of stock of the United States, bearing an Interest of six per Cent, to our son Henry Alex. Desaussure, who holds the same in Trust for his mother. For which sum we have sent on a duplicate receipt. The Credit is to take effect as of the 1st day of July 1816. The stock remitted was for the sum of Two thousand, six hundred & ninety eight dollars, 77 cents, which being taken at 92 1/2 per Cent, makes the sum to be credited $2496 36/100 as above Stated.

August 5. 1816. Henry Wm. DeSaussure
Eliza: DeSaussure

Gab. H. Ford to H. W. Desaussure Bond
See payment within

Receipt to Gabriel Ford from his sister and brother-in-law for $2,496.36 in stock, which Gabriel paid to his nephew in trust for his mother—Gabriel's sister. *Morristown National Historical Park.*

No. 114

This is to Certify, that Gabriel H. Ford Esqr
of the Township of Morris in the county of Morris
in the second collection district of New-Jersey, has paid the duty of four dollars for the year ending the 31st day of December eighteen hundred and fourteen for, and upon a two wheel carriage, for the conveyance of persons, hanging on steel springs called a riding chair owned by himself

This certificate to be of no avail any longer than the aforesaid carriage shall be owned by the said Gabriel H. Ford unless said certificate shall be produced to the Collector by whom it was granted, and an entry be made thereon, specifying the name of the then owner of said carriage, and the time when he or she became possessed thereof.

Given in conformity with an act of the Congress of the United States, passed on the 24th day of July, 1813.

January 17 1814

Edward Condict
Collector of the Revenue for the Second
Collection District of New-Jersey.

No. 115

This is to certify, that Gabriel H. Ford Esqr
of the Township of Morris in the county of Morris
in the second collection district of New-Jersey, has paid the duty of two dollars for the year ending the 31st day of December eighteen hundred and fourteen for, and upon a Two wheel carriage, for the conveyance of persons, hanging on wooden springs called a sulkey owned by himself

This certificate to be of no avail any longer than the aforesaid carriage shall be owned by the said Gabriel H. Ford unless said certificate shall be produced to the Collector by whom it was granted, and an entry be made thereon specifying the name of the then owner of said carriage, and the time when he or she became possessed thereof.

Given in conformity with an act of the Congress of the United States, passed on the 24th day of July, 1813.

January 17 1814

Edward Condict
Collector of the Revenue for the Second
Collection District of New-Jersey.

Receipt to Gabriel Ford for a tax paid on his carriage, January 1814. *Morristown National Historical Park.*

Theodosia Ford saith she is the widow of Col.
Jacob Ford Junr deceased, who died the day of
January 1777, leaving by her five children, to wit,
Timothy, born December 1763; Gabriel, born Janury 1765,
Elizabeth born and married afterward
to Henry Wm DeSaussure; Jacob, born
& Phebe born who died under four years
old; That the provision in her husband's will in
lieu of her Dower she accepted
That she remembers to have heard of the sale of
some of her husband's forges and rough lands after
his death to John Jacob Faesch; but never understood that Moses Tuttle had any part of the said land
or was to pay the estate for it until within one or two years past; nor any conversation like
it among any of her surviving children
though they continued members of her family always till they married or went into business, excepting absences at College & for the purposes of
education. She also says
the father of her husband died in about a week
after his said Son: that the Revd Timothy Johnes
her father minister of the Gospel was settled at
Morristown, and according to the best of her belief
she thinks his knowledge of Iron works and rough
mountain lands about Mount Pleasant, the Middle
forge, and Burnt Meadow, and the values thereof
was exceedingly limited and vague: that Moses Tuttle
has been the owner or conductor of iron works at Mount-
Pleasant or near that place ever since she
member him there which is
ago, and
how much longer she cannot tell: that he was
always esteemed by her husband and she thinks
by most of other people for his understanding &
good judgment

& Phebe born
old; That the provision in her husband's will in
lieu of her Dower she accepted
That she remembers to have heard of the sale of
some of her husband's forges and rough lands after
his death to John Jacob Faesch; but never understood that Moses Tuttle had any part of the said land
or was to pay the estate for it until within one or two years past; nor any conversation like
it among any of her surviving children
though they continued members of her family always till they married or went into business, excepting absences at College & for the purposes of
education. She also says
the father of her husband died in about a week
after his said Son: that the Revd Timothy Johnes
her father minister of the Gospel was settled at
Morristown, and according to the best of her belief
she thinks his knowledge of Iron works and rough
mountain lands about Mount Pleasant, the Middle
forge, and Burnt Meadow, and the values thereof
was exceedingly limited and vague: that Moses Tuttle
has been the owner or conductor of iron works at Mount-
Pleasant or near that place ever since she
member him there which is
ago, and
how much longer she cannot tell: that he was
always esteemed by her husband and she thinks
by most of other people for his understanding &
good judgment in matters of business: She is sure
from a memorandum of her own making at the
time that a certain sum of Eleven hundred & fifteen
dollars continental money equal to £446 York money
was paid to her by Moses Tuttle on the twelfth day
of February 1779.

Affidavit from Theodosia Ford in a case against Moses Tuttle concerning her late husband's forges, 1779. *Morristown National Historical Park.*

Mrs. Ford seems to fade into the background after the Revolution. There are occasional glimpses of her but never anything of substance enough to feel her presence directly. She unfortunately—and maybe by choice—is an indirect historical figure due to the lack of information. From the handful of references to her that do exist, though, she can be seen as having had a disproportionately enormous impact on the history of the Ford Mansion. She lived in the mansion with her family until her death in 1826, when she was laid to rest beside her husband, Jacob Ford Jr., in the Morristown Presbyterian cemetery, next to the church at which her father had once been pastor.

GABRIEL FORD

The nineteenth-century history of the mansion, prior to the Washington Association of New Jersey in 1873, is dominated by the figure of Gabriel Ford and his son Henry. Gabriel (1765–1849), the second-eldest child of Jacob and Theodosia, graduated from Princeton in 1784 and became an attorney in 1789. He had a distinguished legal career serving as a judge on the Morris County Court of Common Pleas, and from 1820 to 1840 as a justice on the New Jersey Supreme Court. Much like his parents, Gabriel seems to have not used the mansion as a place for excessive social entertaining. There are no stories or reports of the mansion being the social center of Morristown. Society life of any type was not for Gabriel Ford; he did not even feel that colleges were suitable places. His sons attended private academies before being tutored by Gabriel in the law.[128]

Gabriel acted as the Ford family attorney, overseeing the family's business and agricultural interests. He kept the family business interest in the Hibernia mine profitable, and he litigated numerous land disputes involving his father's executors and land connected to the forges. The disputes between the Ford family and other mine operators took on an even more serious tone set against the backdrop of the overall decline of the industry in New Jersey. With their livelihood being threatened by the discovery of iron in the Great Lakes region, the last thing New Jersey mine owners needed was internecine legal battles.

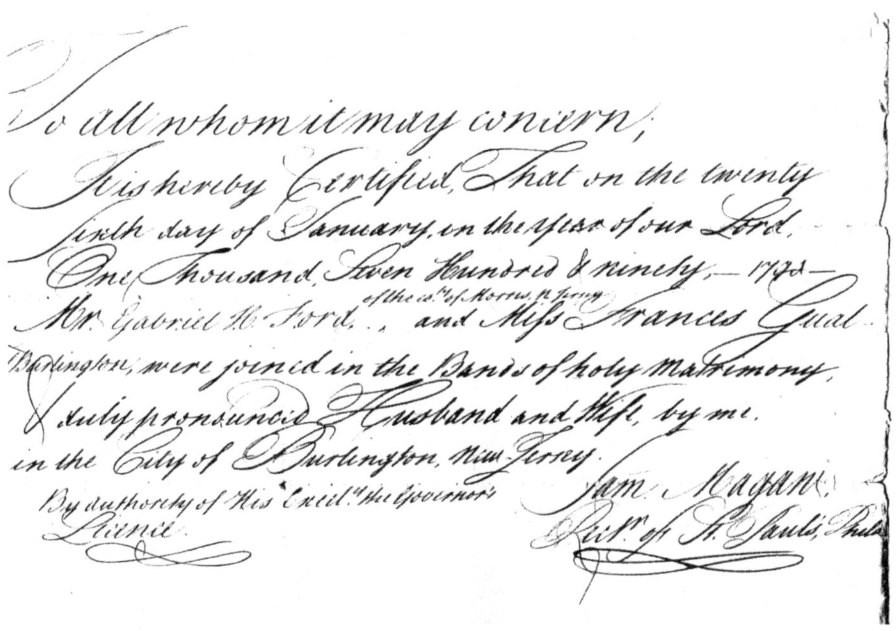
To all whom it may concern;
It is hereby Certified, That on the twenty sixth day of January, in the Year of our Lord, One Thousand, Seven Hundred & ninety,—1790—
Mr. Gabriel H. Ford, of the Co. of Morris, N. Jersey, and Miss Frances Gual. Burlington, were joined in the Bands of holy Matrimony, & duly pronounced Husband and Wife, by me, in the City of Burlington, New Jersey.
By authority of His Excel.cy the Governor's Licence.
Sam. Magaw, Rect.r of St. Paul's Phila

Marriage certificate of Gabriel Ford and Frances Burlington, January 26, 1791. *Morristown National Historical Park.*

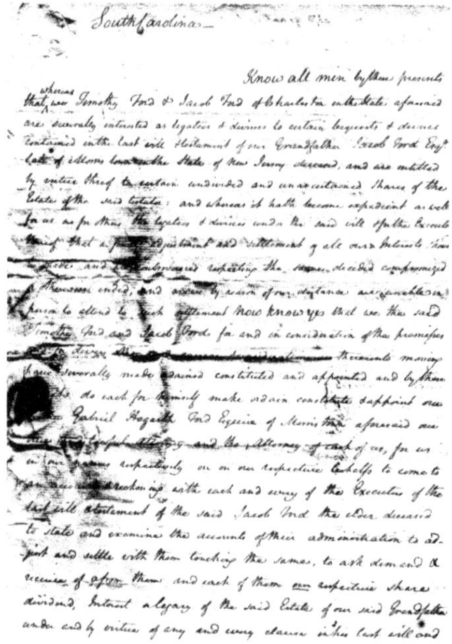

South Carolina —

Know all men by these presents that whereas we Timothy Ford & Jacob Ford of Charleston in the State aforesaid are severally entitled as legatees & devisees to certain bequests & devises contained in the last will & testament of our Grandfather Jacob Ford Esqr late of Morristown in the State of New Jersey deceased, and are entitled by virtue thereof to certain undivided and unascertained shares of the Estate of the said testator: and whereas it hath become expedient ...

Timothy Ford and Jacob Ford III appointing their brother Gabriel to power of attorney, circa 1800. *Morristown National Historical Park.*

Page of account book of Gabriel Ford showing payments to John Jacob Faesch, 1793–96. *Morristown National Historical Park.*

With the further decline of the iron industry, the Fords—Mrs. Ford, Gabriel, his wife Frances and their children—shifted the emphasis more and more to the farm portion of the family business. Gabriel had his lucrative legal career, too, which helped to supplement the declining revenue from the iron industry. By 1830, after his mother's death, Gabriel seems to have shifted the base of the family's wealth conclusively from iron to legal services primarily and farming secondarily.

What remained of the family iron business was increasingly being run by other family members and effectively ceased being a major interest or source of income for the children of Jacob Ford Jr. by about 1830. The iron industry, once the bedrock of New Jersey's prominence, was overtaken by cheaper iron produced in the new lands opening in the west, particularly in the Great Lakes region.

Furthermore, the financial depression of 1837 would have also played some negative role in the restructuring of the commercial business related ventures of the Fords. The 1837 depression was one of the first severe national financial crisis. It was one of the reasons why President Martin Van Buren was defeated for a second term in 1840. This switch led to a decline in the overall financial status of the Ford family. Though by no means destitute, the family

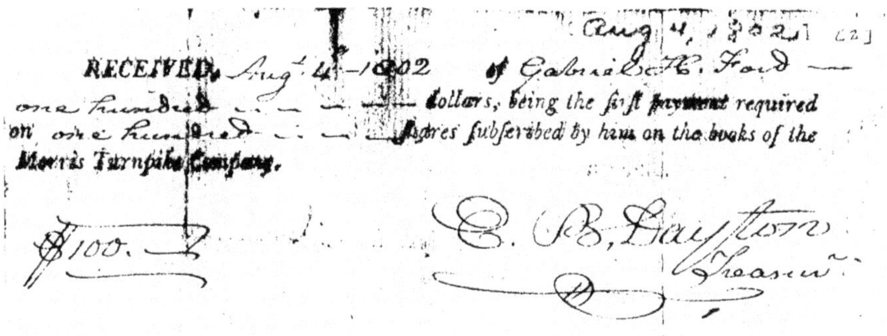

Aug 4, 1802

RECEIVED, Aug 4 -1802 of Gabriel H. Ford — one hundred — dollars, being the first payment required on one hundred shares subscribed by him on the books of the Morris Turnpike Company.

$100.

E. B. Dayton, Treasr.

Receipt for one hundred shares of Morris County Turnpike stock for Gabriel Ford, 1802. *Morristown National Historical Park.*

under Gabriel seems to have moved beyond the early industrial generators of wealth (iron) and into the service sector (law) as the Fords deftly learned to accommodate and manipulate the larger commercial and industrialization trends of the state of New Jersey during the mid-nineteenth century.

As with any economy based too extensively on natural resources, this was not always advisable, as there is always the possibility of depleting those resources and thus jeopardizing the economic foundation. This was in danger of happening: "By the late 1700s in New Jersey, considerable depletion of natural resources had occurred."[129] Several decades into the nineteenth century, the situation was even worse.

The Mansion's Development in the Nineteenth Century

During the forty-six years following Washington's departure in 1780 and Mrs. Ford's death in 1826, the mansion and grounds experienced minimal changes. Those that occurred prior to about 1815 were all generally of a utilitarian nature. An 1804 survey of the Ford farmlands indicated meadows and cleared land across the street and an orchard and woodlands to the north. There were also three outbuildings: a stable, a barn and a farmhouse.[130] Several other structures, too, were built by Gabriel during the first quarter of the nineteenth century. These buildings included a wagon house, a smokehouse, a stone cistern and a milk house. An icehouse and a root cellar were also in place by 1850. As can be seen, the Ford family farm was apparently thriving during the nineteenth century.

Gu

***YOUR** Policy of Assurance, No.* 320641 *issued from this Office, will expire at 6 o'clock, of the Evening of the* 21 *day of* March *next; the Premium for the renewal of which, amounting to $* 5 82/100 *must be paid on or before such period, otherwise the Policy will be void.*

***THOMAS W. SATTERTHWAITE**, Agent.*

London Phoenix Fire Office
No. 26 WALL-STREET,
OPPOSITE THE MERCHANTS' BANK,
NEW-YORK:
the 26 day of Feb 1814

N. B. the Office does not take upon itself to be responsible for sending notices, or for their delivery, but it will be done as far as practicable.

TO PERSONS INSURED.

Persons insured are desired to take notice, that although fifteen days, af[illegible] gular expiration of the Policies, are allowed for the renewal of the same, the office is not responsible for any loss which may occur during such days of grace, unless previously thereto the premium has been duly paid, and that in case of neglect beyond the period in question, the insurance can be continued only by a new Policy.

The Assured in this office are hereby informed, that the validity of Policies issued in this Agency, is no way affected by the present war; and that the Company will, as heretofore, most scrupulously adhere to their obligations. The Agent has been expressly directed by the Board of Directors in London, to make this declaration. Sufferers will experience all possible promptitude and honor in the adjustment and discharge of claims.

Notice of insurance renewal to Gabriel Ford—presumably for the mansion, February 1814. *Morristown National Historic Park.*

Evidence shows the front yard as having been fenced in by 1790, at about the same time that poplar trees were planted in the front lawn.[131] Gabriel Ford, who acquired full ownership of the mansion and grounds in 1805, "had considerable interest in gardening and horticulture and was personally involved in the design and planting of his grounds."[132] Gabriel planted a mixture of native and nonnative trees, including "horse chestnut, mountain ash, larch, locust, linden, hawthorn, pear, and weeping

Depiction of Morristown, circa 1850. *Morristown National Historical Park.*

willow."[133] Gabriel planted potatoes in the front yard and had continued to add ornamentals to the grounds through the 1820s (see appendix 1). The most long-term impact to the grounds, though, occurred before 1850 when the Morris and Essex Railroad cut across a southern portion of the Ford property, thus severing the estate and heralding a new threat to the continuity of the estate—subdivision.[134]

After Gabriel's death in 1849, the mansion passed to his son, Henry, who did little to alter the property left to him by his father. The landscape, which was so important to Gabriel as the focus of the Ford family's heritage, held little interest for Henry (see appendix 2). He rather "maintained the grounds as left by his father rather than continuing to further enhance the landscape."[135] Henry was more practical in his approach to the ownership of the mansion and less centered on the appearance of the estate. In 1860, he applied for fire insurance with the Rahway Mutual Fire Insurance Company and generally maintained the property instead of improving it (see appendix 3).

The Postwar Growth of New Jersey

Post–Revolutionary War New Jersey, from an economic standpoint, was much like it was in the prewar years. New Jersey was still predominantly agricultural and continued to attract a diverse number of immigrants. Even as late as 1834, a writer in the *Gazetteer of the State of New Jersey* wrote that "the state is, in the aggregate, agricultural…The glass and iron manufactures…are not sufficient to exempt them from this classification."[136] As one traveler noted in 1806, "New Jersey is settled with frugal, industrious farmers. The produce of the state…and a vast quantity of fruit…for the supply of the New York and Philadelphia markets."[137] In Morris County, the labor force included hired laborers, indentured servants and slaves.[138] It is known that Gabriel relied on slave labor and indentured servants until 1825. While he did not own slaves directly, Gabriel, and his parents, often hired their services from other owners. Gabriel Ford even mentions a slave belonging to his mother going by the name of Pompey.[139] The full extent of the family's use of slaves is unclear. Overall, New Jersey law allowed for manumission in 1804 and outlawed slavery in 1846.[140]

New Jersey also faced other challenges during this period. For years prior to 1840, during the first quarter of the nineteenth century, the state overall experienced immigration of citizens to western areas of the country as the region opened to settlement. Areas such as Kentucky, Tennessee, Indiana, Ohio and Illinois all benefited from the immigration of New Jersey residents into their more fertile agricultural lands. By 1840, however, the trend began to reverse, as more New Jersey residents chose to stay in the state and take advantage of the new opportunities provided by the developing industrial economy.

By mid-century, New Jersey had a permanently established city-based manufacturing working class.[141] This was generally concentrated in the northern areas and to the east toward New York. Southern New Jersey still remained heavily agricultural and sparsely populated. The 1830 New Jersey population was 320,000; in 1860 it was 672,000. Seven new counties were created to deal with the increased population politically. Although still highly agricultural, the Industrial Revolution was slowly transforming New Jersey economically and demographically. During the mid-nineteenth century, a vast majority of the immigrants were Irish, and by 1880, this had shifted to Italians and Poles.[142]

Transportation advances ensured New Jersey's continued access to both New York and Philadelphia. The county road near the Ford Mansion to

Newark and Elizabethtown was enlarged and upgraded in the early 1800s, which ensured Morristown's prominence as a major route in the area.[143] In all, "The state legislature chartered fifty-one turnpikes in the period between 1801 and 1829, nearly all of them north of a line between Burlington and Perth Amboy."[144] Taken together, "About 550 miles of more-or-less improved toll roadways reached through much of North Jersey before the turnpike rash subsided."[145] The New Jersey Turnpike, which is still in use today, was one of these early toll roads. In addition to land transportation, water transport was becoming increasingly economical by 1825. Morristown resident George Macculloch developed the idea for the Morris Canal, which was built between 1824 and 1834 across the northern tip of Morris County, thus linking Pennsylvania with New York harbors.[146] The "canal gave the North Jersey hills an economic boost that persisted for decades."[147]

Immediately following the canal system was the railroad. "The New Jersey Railroad company received its charter in 1832," although it was naturally heavily opposed by the canal companies.[148] Because the Morris and Essex Railroad began operation in 1835, Morristown, Morris County and northern New Jersey were all well prepared to embrace the further development of the industrial trades. Railroads transformed the state in ways few could have imagined. The opportunities existed in abundance in certain areas. With access to western raw materials and western markets, New Jersey flourished in its place along with most of the rest of the East Coast.

While still attracting immigrants, a large portion of New Jersey's population came from families who had considered New Jersey home for several generations by 1850. The large number of inherited properties, particularly farmland, suggests a stable social and economic environment.[149] Some traditional agricultural patterns established prior to the war were still in use at the turn of the nineteenth century.

The Final Chapter of Ford Family Ownership

Gabriel's son Henry (1793–1872), the last Ford to own the mansion, continued in his father's chosen path of law. Henry, however, became more involved in civil affairs on the local, state and national level. He and his wife, Jane Hosack Millen, had twelve children, and part of the family moved on a part-time basis into the mansion upon the death of Gabriel in 1849, even though they already had an established home of their own. Through Gabriel's will a large quantity of Ford land surrounding the mansion was

Above, left: Death inventory of Mrs. Gabriel Ford. *Morristown National Historical Park.*

Above, right: Mrs. Gabriel Ford's death inventory, with mention of George Washington. *Morristown National Historical Park.*

sold to developers, and Henry primarily maintained the areas immediately adjacent to the mansion. Henry's mother, Frances, was also residing at the mansion as she had life tenancy through Gabriel's will.

Henry and his large family did not live full time at the mansion as he was already fifty-seven and his children were mostly grown with their own families. The mansion was leased to various in-laws and was no longer the scene of a full-time Ford occupant. Henry, and his mother until her death in 1853, continued to run the farming activities until about 1855, when for all intents and purposes the Ford family farms ceased to operate on a large scale for revenue purposes.

After Gabriel's death in 1849, the living connection to the Washington period was severed. Henry seems to have had little of the sense of the mansion as a shrine and continued to sell off parcels of property for development. Much as the railroad bisecting Gabriel's estate foreshadowed the future breakup of the property, Henry Ford looked to the estate as a commodity. It was something in which to invest, or sell outright, to improve the financial status of the owner. The concept of history seemed not to bother him. Henry Ford and his children thus passed into New Jersey's booming industrial economy with little apparent interest in the past. New Jersey, and indeed the American outlook, was decidedly geared toward the future.

When Henry A. Ford died in 1872, his will called for the subdivision of the property and for the entire estate, including the mansion, to be sold at auction to the highest bidder. The proceeds were to be divided among his children. The idea of preservation was clearly not on his mind. Most of his children were already established and had no need for such an "old-fashioned" home. In fact, one of Henry's sons, Henry W. Ford, had built a stylish Second Empire mansion of his own within sight of the old family homestead. While the Washington connection was certainly known within the family, it seemed not to matter in terms of the potential income the estate could generate through a sale.

The major problem with finding a buyer for the mansion was finding someone who was interested in the old-fashioned styling of the architecture. By 1873, the Romantic Revival style dominated the new houses of the

Henry A. Ford mansion, located across the street from the Jacob Ford Mansion, circa 1885, razed in the early twentieth century. *Morristown National Historical Park.*

upper classes. The style was even modified downward so the middle-class homeowner could afford a home in the latest fashion. The Ford Mansion, alas, stuck out like a "sore thumb" architecturally against the new tastes described as Gothic Revival, Italianate, Second Empire and Queen Anne.[150] Some of the patterns were even mixed and matched, creating something quite bohemian and something the staid Ford Mansion could never aspire to.

News of the terms of the will did, however, create intense interest from a small but dedicated group of preservationists. As the date of the auction neared, newspapers were actually leading the charge for the preservation of the mansion. One wrote, "The sacred associations of our Revolutionary days ought to secure a large and appreciative attendance."[151]

THE OUTCRY

The auction firm of Betts, Burnett, and Company handled the business arrangements for the auction scheduled for June 28, 1873. The announcement for the sale stated:

> *The estate and residence known as the Headquarters of the late General Washington is to be sold to that citizen, soldier, or statesman who desires to become successor of the Father of his country in its occupation. Or it can be made one of the finest hotels or fashionable resorts in the state.*[152]

The twin inducements of patriotism and financial reward are clearly joined in an effort by the auction house to lure potential bidders. Missing, of course, is any mention of the mansion as a home. It had outlived its usefulness for this purpose and could only now be a shrine frozen in time or a moneymaking venture in which a quaint, old-fashioned visit beckoned visitors worn out with the modern world. Either way, the mansion's future laid in its past.

The *Elizabeth Daily Herald* seemed to capture the mood of most New Jerseyans with an article from early 1873 after the sale was announced. "The article bemoaned the American public for its apparent lack of concern for the future of the mansion and all that it represented. Much of the commentary is tinged with cynicism resulting from the anxiety of a nation still reeling from the turmoil of a bloody civil war."[153] The horrors of the Civil War tended to cause people to look back to a more glorious past,

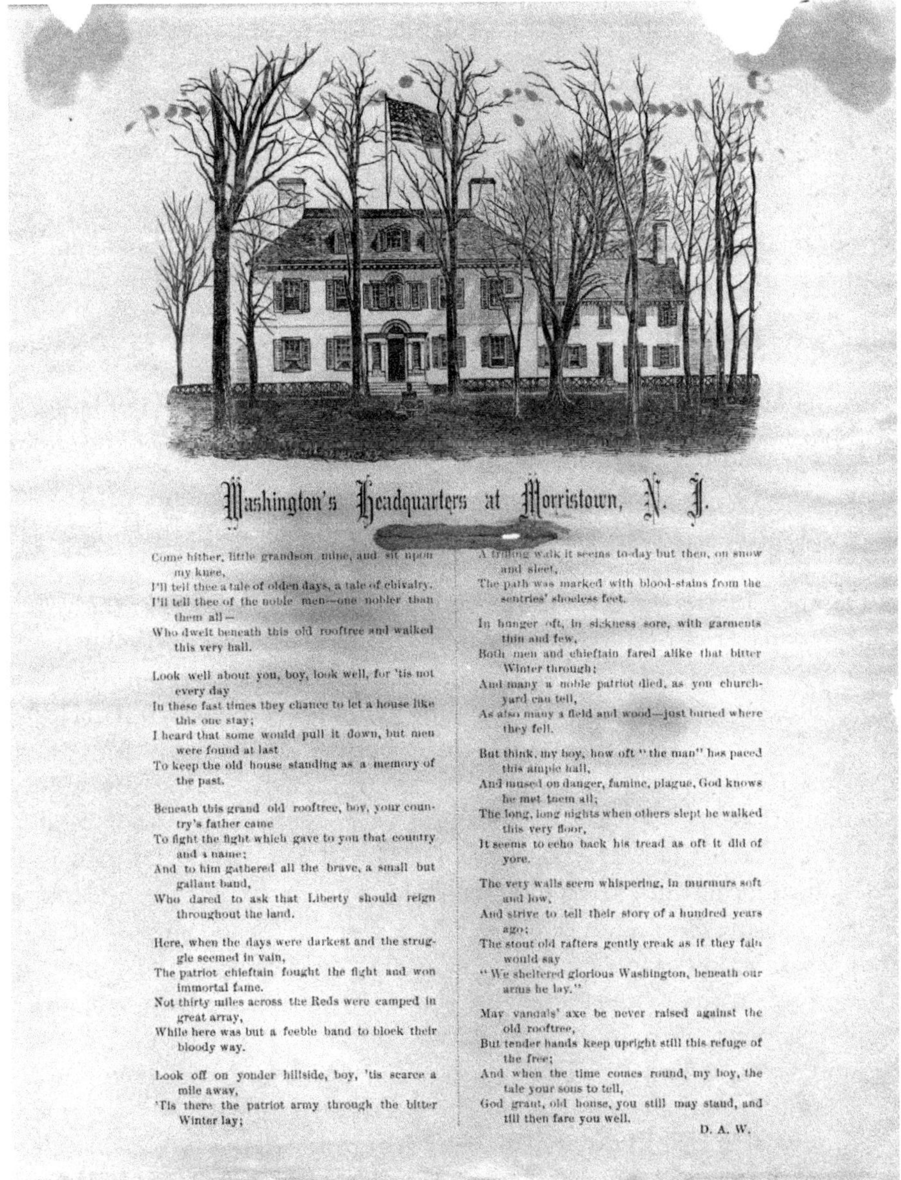

Washington's Headquarters at Morristown, N. J.

Come hither, little grandson mine, and sit upon my knee,
I'll tell thee a tale of olden days, a tale of chivalry.
I'll tell thee of the noble men—one nobler than them all—
Who dwelt beneath this old rooftree and walked this very hall.

Look well about you, boy, look well, for 'tis not every day
In these fast times they chance to let a house like this one stay;
I heard that some would pull it down, but men were found at last
To keep the old house standing as a memory of the past.

Beneath this grand old rooftree, boy, your country's father came
To fight the fight which gave to you that country and a name;
And to him gathered all the brave, a small but gallant band,
Who dared to ask that Liberty should reign throughout the land.

Here, when the days were darkest and the struggle seemed in vain,
The patriot chieftain fought the fight and won immortal fame.
Not thirty miles across the Reds were camped in great array,
While here was but a feeble band to block their bloody way.

Look off on yonder hillside, boy, 'tis scarce a mile away,
'Tis there the patriot army through the bitter Winter lay;
A trifling walk it seems to-day but then, on snow and sleet,
The path was marked with blood-stains from the sentries' shoeless feet.

In hunger oft, in sickness sore, with garments thin and few,
Both men and chieftain fared alike that bitter Winter through;
And many a noble patriot died, as yon churchyard can tell,
As also many a field and wood—just buried where they fell.

But think, my boy, how oft "the man" has paced this ample hall,
And mused on danger, famine, plague, God knows he met them all;
The long, long nights when others slept he walked this very floor,
It seems to echo back his tread as oft it did of yore.

The very walls seem whispering, in murmurs soft and low,
And strive to tell their story of a hundred years ago;
The stout old rafters gently creak as if they fain would say
"We sheltered glorious Washington, beneath our arms he lay."

May vandals' axe be never raised against the old rooftree,
But tender hands keep upright still this refuge of the free;
And when the time comes round, my boy, the tale your sons to tell,
God grant, old house, you still may stand, and till then fare you well.

D. A. W.

An 1876 poem about the Ford Mansion. *Morristown National Historical Park.*

and the upcoming American centennial in 1876 was also stoking patriotic feelings (see appendix 4).

In all of the discussions that preceded the sale, no mention of the Ford family descendants and their apparent lack of concern about the fate of their ancestral home was made. Many, however, felt that money was behind the sale. One editor in the *Newark Daily Advertiser* wrote, "It is presumed that pecuniary circumstances [have] prompted the owner to dispose of it in this manner."[154]

REMEMBERING THE MANSION

The Ford Mansion, far from being forgotten in this climate, was actually remembered in its own right and was the recipient of attention fostered by larger societal forces. These forces would ultimately affect the field of historic preservation over the next several decades.[155]

The mansion received some measure of public recognition in the years that predated and postdated the sale in 1873. It was featured in Benson Lessing's 1851 work *The Pictorial Field Book of the Revolution* and in *Appleton's Journal* in 1874 (after the sale, but when the mansion's future was still unclear) in an article called "Washington's Headquarters at Morristown."[156] The mansion had been featured in an 1859 article in *Harper's Weekly*, as well as other more local periodicals and books, such as those by local historians John Barber and Henry Home, who wrote in 1844.[157] The mansion naturally was well known locally and had a high recognition factor among area residents. Throughout the nineteenth century, the mansion was nearly always referred to as "Washington's Headquarters" on local maps. Furthermore, a thriving trade in postcards that featured the mansion during the early twentieth century helped to introduce the Ford Mansion beyond New Jersey. Even the encampment sites in Jockey Hollow were remembered through a mixture of local history and legend. Certain sites in Morristown were already venerated as historical shrines prior to the establishment of the park.[158]

A nationwide grass-roots effort at preservation began with the Washington's Headquarters in Newburgh, New York, which was saved in 1850. The Washington site above all others, Mount Vernon, was organized as a historic site in 1853 by the Mount Vernon Ladies Association.

CHAPTER 5

The Washington Association of New Jersey

The Auction

The day of the auction was a huge social event. The Morristown *True Democratic Banner* provided a glimpse of the festivities:

> [A] *special train arrived from New York and unloaded about 300 persons who immediately started in body for the Headquarters to partake of the lunch…Four flags hung from the front of the property, while over the front door of the mansion stood Fairchild's life-like portrait of Washington… At half past one the sale of lots commenced…Of the 47 lots laid out, nineteen were put up and claimed to be sold aggregating the amount of $44,310.50…The Headquarters property was then put up, and immediately the liveliest interest was manifested.*[159]

When the bidding on the mansion and estate reached $24,100, "ex-governor Randolph…stepped into the open space before the auctioneer" and offered to purchase the site for $25,000 if three others would join him.[160] "Uproarious applause followed this surprise…and Washington's Headquarters was knocked down to Morristown and Newark patriotism."[161]

At the sale on June 25, 1873, four New Jersey businessmen came together and purchased the mansion and the remaining estate grounds. The four were Theodore Randolph (a former New Jersey governor), General Nathaniel Norris Halsted (a prosperous dry goods merchant), Honorable George Halsey (of the New Jersey Historical Society) and

Clockwise, from top left:
William van Vleck Lidgerwood, WANJ founder. *Morristown National Historical Park.*
Theodore Randolph, WANJ founder. *Morristown National Historical Park.*
Nathaniel Halsted, Washington Association of New Jersey (WANJ) founder. *Morristown National Historical Park.*
George Halsey, WANJ founder. *Morristown National Historical Park.*

William van Vleck Lidgerwood (a wealthy businessman who grew up in Morristown).[162]

It is highly unlikely that the scene as described was a "spontaneous" event.[163] The men knew each other and their interests. As is mostly the pattern concerning the mansion, there is little evidence to suggest the motivation of Randolph and his new partners. It is unknown whether they conspired prior to Randolph's dramatic bid. There is no mention of the inspiration for his actions or whether he was impressed with the work of the preservation initiatives of the Mount Vernon Ladies Association. One of the four initial buyers, Nathaniel Halsted, was also connected with the Mount Vernon restoration. His wife, Nancy Halsted, was the New Jersey vice-regent for the Mount Vernon Ladies Association. Whether Mrs. Halsted provided inspiration for her husband is unknown, but given the exclusion of women from membership in the Washington Association of New Jersey (WANJ) that emerged later, it seems unlikely that she had much impact. The four were each very wealthy and very well connected politically. This pattern of wealth and political connections was to be quickly replicated in the membership of the WANJ as it began operation. "A comparison of members of elite clubs in the Morristown area whose names are given in local histories with the WANJ membership list shows that a high proportion of the men belonged to the WANJ" too.[164]

It would also seem that historic preservation, as a concept, was merely an unintended by-product of the purchase. Randolph and his partners did not fit the role of the traditional preservationist in late nineteenth-century America, when it was still predominately a woman's purview. Whatever the motivation, "The auction of the Ford Mansion marked a minor (although significant) milestone in the history of the preservation movement in America….the public attention to the sale of the mansion is notable due to the fact that little concern had been shown for America's national history prior to the Centennial exhibition in Philadelphia three years later."[165]

Randolph, Lidgerwood, Halsey and Halsted had gathered "a good amount of respect and public trust for their cavalier efforts to save the mansion, and to this sentiment they sought to build its secure future."[166] In an open letter printed on September 29, 1873, Randolph wrote that the new association's object "was to keep the place from being desecrated by passing into the hands of improper or speculative persons."[167] Randolph further asked his fellow New Jerseyans "if you think the object a worthy one, and desire to contribute to it, or know of any one who may deem it a privilege to be connected with such an association, I will be glad, as either of my associates will, to receive your subscriptions."[168] The biggest shock for Randolph came when he found out that the state legislature would not take over responsibility for the mansion. Randolph had hoped that the state would agree to public funding to financially stabilize the investment that he and his three associates had made. Without large amounts of public money from the state, Randolph had to resort to forming a semipublic club organization supported by its members through subscription memberships.

THE WASHINGTON ASSOCIATION OF NEW JERSEY BEGINS

The new Washington Association secured an act of incorporation from the state legislature on March 20, 1874. The organizational structure of the association was "neither entirely independent nor dependent on the State."[169] The agreement allowed for the state to provide modest funding for care and maintenance, while the association would have the structure "open to the public, free of charge, at all proper times" for visitation.[170] The unique nature of this collaborative effort would eventually see the state becoming the largest shareholder in the association by 1930. Membership was only for men and was only through stock purchase, which could only be inherited by a male descendant. Women could purchase shares and fundraise but not inherit shares. Women were granted membership status in 1946. Under its bylaws, if a member died without a male heir, that interest devolved to the State of New Jersey. By the time of the transfer of the mansion to the NPS in 1933, the large number of shares owned by New Jersey virtually guaranteed that the transfer would occur.

In 1875, a new amendment to the state constitution caused the state subsidies to be rescinded. This loss of state funding was a sharp blow to the young association. Between trying to stabilize their financial situation and seeking to structurally stabilize the mansion, the association was put to the test early on in its existence. Within three years, though, the state subsidy was restored, and the association finally began to enjoy some measure of stability and success. By the mid-1880s, the association began to expand by the acquisition of small adjoining plots and by expanding the museum collection. A caretaker's cottage was built, or moved to the site, and the landscape was improved.

Protecting the estate from residential development near the mansion became a major goal during the 1880s. The WANJ bought up as much of the former Henry Ford estate as possible to ensure a buffer around the mansion.

"After each purchase, the new property was graded and landscaped to match the immediate landscape of the mansion."[171] The association's plan for the landscape was to create "one of the most beautiful spots in New Jersey."[172] It "planted hundreds of shade and evergreen trees and shrubs."[173]

The Development of an Ideal

With the creation of the Washington Association of New Jersey, the mansion entered an entirely new period of its existence. As former governor and WANJ founder Theodore Randolph remarked to an assembled audience in 1875:

> *The same oaken doors open to you as they did to Washington; the knocker his hand was wont to touch yet waits obedient to your wish, floors he trod in anxious thought and with wearied brain, you may tread. The century has wrought no change in rafter or beam, or floor, or sheltering oak. Is there no significance in the remarkable preservation of this house?*
>
> *This dwelling was for many months the home of Martha, the wife of George Washington. Within these rooms, with quiet dignity and grace, she received her husband's guests. Never idle, she set a constant example of thrift and industry…*
>
> *The curious old secretary he used, with its hidden drawers and quaint workmanship, stands here now as it did then. The mirrors used by General and Lady Washington you may see your faces reflected in. The old camp chest, heavy and solid, is yet good for a long campaign.*[174]

The purpose of the mansion had surely changed. No longer was it a residence or a home; it had become a shrine. It was now a memorial not just to Washington, but also to the entire forgotten period of the eighteenth century that produced such a structure. It was also a memorial to the direct role the mansion played in the Revolutionary period. This change occurred virtually overnight, and with it the mansion immediately became a destination spot for visitors. With the organizational structure of the association fully in place by 1875, when Randolph spoke, the disorganization and uncertainty of 1873 seemed like a century ago. Randolph and his colleagues had in two short, tense years charted a new path for heritage tourism.

Corresponding nicely with the creation of the historic shrine at the mansion by the WANJ was the arrival of new types of "migrants" to the Morris

County area. Prior to the Civil War, but more generally after it, "Morristown and its environs...emerged not only as a destination for visitors attracted by its healthy climate and pastoral surroundings, but more importantly as a place of large country estates."[175] Wealthy New Yorkers began to move to the Morris County area to escape the teeming crowds of the city. Land was plentiful and inexpensive, and Morris County was close enough to the city to allow for a weekly commute. As with the vast majority of the Ford estate property, "Land use and settlement patterns changed as marginal farmlands were abandoned, and small farms were consolidated into large estates."[176] The industrial and commercial changes that were sweeping New Jersey and the nation after the Civil War also greatly affected land use. As more and more commercial tradesmen moved to a fixed out-of-the-home office (Henry A. Ford was the first Ford to keep an office downtown) or workspace, they inevitably created a more vibrant and expanded commercial district. As this grew, more farmland became susceptible to being turned to other uses besides agriculture. The Ford property represented something of a reversal of the trend, though, in that a large estate was subdivided into smaller parcels for houses, not for farms.

DEVELOPING THE MANSION'S NEW ROLE

The mansion quickly became a magnet for virtually every type of memento from Morristown, whether it had historical merit or not. Many of the artifacts that came with a Washington connection attached were, in fact, not at all associated with Washington. To this day, the collection at the Morristown National Historical Park (the subject of the next chapter), which acquired the WANJ collection, is full of items that are described as "believed to have been" or "thought to have been" somehow associated with Washington, either George or Martha. Even beyond the Revolutionary period, many donors felt the need to donate Civil War–era items, as well as items from earlier in the nineteenth century and into the twentieth.

One of Henry Ford's daughters, Mrs. Canfield, was agreeable to leaving several original Washington items in the mansion. These few pieces, with a direct connection to Washington and 1779, formed the basis of the collection that the association felt was necessary to complete the atmosphere of the mansion's interior.[177]

While most of the more reputable Washington-connected pieces from the mansion were sold at the 1873 auction, the WANJ did manage to purchase

Illustration of Ford Mansion, circa 1885. *Morristown National Historical Park.*

First floor main hall of Ford Mansion, looking north, circa 1920. *Morristown National Historical Park.*

Front hall of Ford Mansion, looking north, 1939, showing some of the WANJ exhibits. *Historic American Buildings Survey.*

East wall outside of kitchen in the Ford Mansion, circa 1920. *Morristown National Historical Park.*

Dining room of the Ford Mansion, circa 1920. *Morristown National Historical Park.*

Second floor of the Ford Mansion with an armory exhibit, circa 1920. *Morristown National Historical Park.*

The boys' room during the WANJ period. *Morristown National Historical Park.*

Members of the WANJ marching near the Morristown Green, circa 1885. *Morristown National Historical Park.*

period furnishings to decorate the mansion. The WANJ worked closely with dealers E.L. Holbrook and G. Davis, who provided many of the items still seen on display today.

With success came challenges. As the association became more adept at running its organization and in promoting the mansion as a destination point, it found that maintenance on the structure was difficult. Without being able to charge admission as per the agreement with the state, WANJ found itself growing short on operating money by the 1890s. Interest in the mansion was spurred further in 1893, when the New Jersey exhibit at the World's Columbian Exposition in Chicago was a replica of the mansion. Attendance was about ten thousand people per year during the 1890s and the first decade of the twentieth century. To add to the organization's problems, the annual subsidy from the state did not rise over the years and was thus continually diminished by inflation.

After World War I, when the automobile became more common, the mansion began to see visitation over twenty thousand per year. This level

Above: Ford Mansion from southeast, circa 1900. *Morristown National Historical Park.*

Left: Front entryway of Ford Mansion, circa 1925. *Morristown National Historical Park.*

of visitation would ultimately prove unsustainable financially as the stress of that many visitors simply multiplied the problems of the aging mansion. Corresponding to rising visitation was a decrease in active members. Without the possibility of female members, the available pool of potential members dwindled as male descendants lost interest in their fathers' pursuits. Finally, the Wall Street collapse of 1929 nearly wiped out the portfolio of the association. Facing unprecedented financial shortfalls, the association was forced to look to other possibilities to keep the mansion viable as a historic site.

CHAPTER 6

The National Park Service

The National Park Service Is Very Interested

The beginning of the historic preservation movement in the United States is generally attributed to Ann Pamela Cunningham and her inspired effort to rescue Mount Vernon in 1854. Throughout the early years of the preservation movement, women usually led the organization and development.[178] In 1873, when the Washington Association sought to save the Ford Mansion, the roles were reversed. Men, not women, founded the association. Women were specifically prevented from participating in any way, except financially, until 1946.

Probably one of the saddest chapters in preservation nationwide occurred in 1863 when, following a four-year battle, the home of John Hancock was destroyed for development.[179] "Between the 1880s and 1920s, some groups began to resist these attitudes [the freewheeling market destruction of the past] and activities."[180] Ultra-wealthy industrialists like auto magnate Henry Ford and John D. Rockefeller Jr. became beacons for their personal ability to preserve structures from destruction. On a small scale, Lloyd W. Smith would also utilize his considerable resources, which were nowhere near Ford or Rockefeller, to save historically sensitive areas from development.

The 1920s brought nearly overwhelming challenges to the association. As the economy expanded greatly during the decade following World War I, visitation numbers at the mansion rose in reflection of this overall expansion. With the increase in visitation, of course, came all of the problems associated with it, such as needing more staff and continual maintenance and repair of the building and grounds. These expenses, along with the overall decline in membership, produced some very trying situations for the association. "Purchases, maintenance, and salaries climbed inexorably after World War I."[181] What eventually became the final straw in the organization's nearly sixty years of ownership of the mansion was the stock market crash of 1929.

During the late 1920s Morristown mayor Clyde Potts was an enthusiastic supporter of an idea to create a shrine or park at the site of the Jockey Hollow winter encampment of 1779–80. Mayor Potts was driven by economic and patriotic motives. Much like the fear of development at the Ford Mansion site had caused concern among preservationists in the 1870s, fear of development at the open expanse of land known as Jockey Hollow proved the impetus to start the process of preservation of the campsite.

Mayor Potts was not alone in his goal. Lloyd W. Smith and W. Redmond Cross, both highly affluent businessmen with more than a passing interest in history, had also become interested in the Potts idea. The exact sequence of events is not recorded in any detail, but the years between 1930 and 1932 were quite active. Smith and Potts particularly were energetic in promoting their idea. Smith, Cross and Potts informally decided to approach the federal government with the suggestion of making a national site out of Jockey Hollow. Much of the credit for the creation of the park really belongs to W. Redmond Cross. He was the first to approach the National Park Service about actually donating land.

W. Redmond Cross met with NPS assistant director Arthur Demaray on March 23, 1931, to discuss the possible transfer of land for the founding of the new park. Unfortunately, Cross fell further into the morass of the Great Depression. Lloyd Smith, who survived the Depression with his fortune intact thanks to deft investing, by late 1931 had purchased Redmond Cross's portion of Jockey Hollow and was in total ownership of the area, and Cross's involvement ceased. Although Redmond Cross left the equation in late 1931, Lloyd Smith carried on strenuously as the new owner of the Jockey Hollow land. Smith was in full agreement with Cross and Mayor Potts that the land encompassing Jockey Hollow should be a memorial of some type. Smith's approach was in keeping with Cross's original view that the area should be set aside for preservation as a memorial to the Continental army's encampment of 1779–80.

Jockey Hollow in 1779–80 provided an ideal place for the winter encampment of the Continental army during that terrible winter. Its vast open areas and sparse population ensured the space necessary for twelve thousand troops. Also, the area was heavily wooded, and this meant that lumber was readily available for the construction of the army's log hut city. While Washington spent the horrible winter in comfort at the Ford Mansion, the army struggled to maintain itself against overwhelming odds. This winter struggle became the stuff of legend over the years. Now, in the 1920s, this area was threatened with obliteration via development. Mayor Potts was personally appalled by the prospect and as mayor felt the proposals for development to be bad for Morristown. He therefore began to promote his idea of seeing the land set aside for preservation as a historic site.

Around the same time, Lloyd Smith and Mayor Potts approached WANJ about possibly including the mansion in the proposed historical park. Lloyd Smith had already decided to donate Jockey Hollow to the federal, state or county government. Smith, who was a member of the association, felt perhaps that he could persuade the board of directors to consider donating the mansion to be a part of the larger proposed park. He also probably felt that his decision with Jockey Hollow might help induce the WANJ board. Horace Albright, the NPS director, lobbied Smith extensively concerning his proposed donation. Albright wrote Smith: "[I]f the property near Morristown which you have acquired should be administered by a national agency, that agency is the National Park Service."[182] Smith's uncertainty was genuine. In addition to the National Park Service, both the State of New Jersey and the War Department (the agency that traditionally administered military sites) made it known to Smith that they wanted his property if he decided to donate.[183] Eventually, the state realized that it could not afford to maintain the new park, and the War Department also felt that the expense would be too great. Somewhat by default, the NPS became Smith's choice.

The impeccable timing of Mayor Potts, Redmond Cross and Lloyd Smith enabled them to form a nearly perfect match with the National Park Service. The convergence of their efforts was greatly enhanced by desires of Director Horace Albright and the NPS. The NPS had simultaneously been thinking about moving into the historic preservation field. The Morristown proposal provided the NPS with an opportunity to fulfill its goal. Director Albright's first plan was to try to transfer military parks from the War Department to the NPS.[184] After this proved a failure, Albright began to concentrate on the idea of creating new historical parks in the East. "The Park Service had only recently received approval to manage sites relating to American Military History, a professional staff of historians and architects had been assembled… and New Deal funds were soon to be available to provide the necessary labor for restoration and presentation to the public."[185] Albright spent fewer than a dozen years with the NPS, as both deputy director and director, yet his contributions to the field of historic preservation have been compared in importance with those of John D. Rockefeller Jr. and his many preservation projects, particularly at Williamsburg.[186] Albright himself stated that one of his goals was to "go rather heavily into the historical park field."[187]

In addition to Albright's vision of historic preservation, the NPS had hired its first professional historian. Verne Chatelain was a young professor at Peru State University in Nebraska when Albright offered him the job. Chatelain had an expansive view of the NPS and its ability to enter the field of historic preservation. However, he was interested in more than simply preserving buildings. He wrote that the purpose of the NPS should be to "breathe the breath of life into American History for those to whom it has been a dull recital of meaningless facts—to recreate for the average citizen something of the color, the pageantry, and the dignity of our national past."[188] Chatelain further saw the role of historian as "a philosopher because his work is essentially synthetic. He is constantly studying causes and effects, processes, patterns, and cycles, in short, everything connected with the development and relationship of human beings in their environment."[189]

Verne Chatelain proved extremely beneficial to Potts and Smith as they pursued their goal. Chatelain was very excited about the prospect of the creation of a historical park within the NPS. As mentioned, the NPS director Albright was pushing hard to move his agency into the field of historical preservation, and the timing seemed to be uniquely coordinated between all the parties. Events moved in favor of all the parties concerned. The biggest unknown by 1932 was whether the association would agree to turn the mansion over to the NPS. Smith's efforts with the WANJ Board had not been totally successful. The Morristown proposal would prove to be the first time that building restoration would be carried out with an all-NPS staff. The Guerin House, the Wick House and above all the Ford Mansion represented "noteworthy milestones in the annals of historic preservation in America."[190]

Historical Patrimony

On December 29, 1932, Lloyd Smith and Clyde Potts, both association members, went before the executive committee of the association to present their proposal for the turning over of the mansion to the NPS. The executive committee saw the prudence of Potts and Smith's argument from a financial perspective and agreed to the transfer with certain conditions—

the association could not sustain the mansion, and seven steps were agreed to for the transfer to occur:

1. *Congress must enact a bill providing for the proposed park, including the Ford house.* [This was crucial as Congressional involvement moved the park beyond monument status, which can be obtained by simple executive order, which the association felt was a slight to its status.]
2. *The Trustees of the Washington Association must ascertain their right and ability to deed the house, land, and furnishings to the Federal Government.*
3. *The New Jersey Legislature must pass a Bill permitting the transfer.*
4. *The Trustees must agree to the transfer.*
5. *Persuade shareholders to approve overwhelmingly.*
6. *The Trustees must deliver binding deeds to the four separate parcels of land acquired since 1873, together with some form of deed listing the major furnishings of the house.*
7. *The deeds must then be accepted by the secretary of the Interior.*

The shareholders proved difficult to convince to agree to the transfer. NPS director Albright sent NPS historian Chatelain and Albright's special assistant Louis Cramton to work with the shareholders to produce something more agreeable to their concerns. "The greatest concerns on behalf of the shareholders involved the administration and the curatorial management of the mansion."[191]

When President Herbert Hoover signed the legislation creating the park on March 2, 1933, the association still had not voted to turn the mansion over to the NPS. It was not until two months later, on May 8, 1933, that the votes were officially tallied in support of turning the mansion, cash reserves and collection over to the NPS.[192]

After the ceremonies officially opening the park on July 4, 1933, the NPS was faced with the challenge of how to fulfill its twofold mission. The General Plan for 1934 stated that the park's overall goals were:

1. *To preserve for posterity a number of buildings, areas, and articles of Revolutionary War interest in as peaceful and natural atmosphere as possible.*
2. *To use these remains, together with all museum and library material, in developing a pleasurable educational and scenic program for the visitor, as well as courses of study for the student.*[193]

The Town of Morristown
and
The Washington Association of New Jersey
request the honor
of your presence
at the ceremonies dedicating
The Morristown National Historical Park
to
The United States of America
on Tuesday, July 4th 1933
at the
Washington Headquarters, Morristown, N.J.
at two thirty o'clock

Committee
Hon. A. Harry Moore, Honorary Chairman
Frank Bergen, Chairman

Franklin D'Olier	Edward K. Mills
P. H. B. Frelinghuysen	Mrs. Paul Moore
Grey W. Higbie	Clyde Potts
John Kean	Lloyd W. Smith

R. S. V. P.
Grey W. Higbie
Morristown, N.J.

Invitation to the opening of the Morristown National Historic Park, 1933. *Morristown National Historical Park.*

The NPS was committed from the beginning to not only obtain and utilize the Ford Mansion, but also to make use of the large museum collection that the association had accumulated over sixty years. To accommodate the collection in an appropriate setting for visitors, the NPS began to design a purpose-built museum building in which to exhibit the collection. The design, announced on October 2, 1934, was created by the firm of the noted Colonial Revival architect John Russell Pope and called for a building "in a Georgian neoclassical style to recall Washington's Mount Vernon home in Virginia incorporating similar covered arcades, wings, symmetry, and a cupola. Pope also designed the museum to complement and harmonize with the Ford Mansion."[194] Completed as part of a Works Progress Administration project, the museum was dedicated in 1938 and opened to the public in 1939.

In addition to the new museum, the NPS created a central workstation for construction of museum exhibits for eastern parks. This workshop had its first home in Lafayette Hall, an association building adjacent to the Ford Mansion. Funding shortfalls soon forced its sixty staff members to reduce operations, and they ultimately moved out of Lafayette Hall. The structure itself was razed in 1941.

Historic Preservation

Since its inception, the historic preservation movement "was characterized by its reliance on private citizens."[195] Generally, "Private concern for our national patrimony came from…affluent Americans" who on one level represented the most distinguished lineages in the country.[196] This trend in America was completely opposite of the approach of many European countries, where governments began preserving historic sites as early as 1845.[197]

The federal government was never seen as a historic preservation alternative. By 1933, the federal government maintained expansive natural wonders such as the Grand Canyon and Yosemite. Additionally, the War Department maintained scenes of military importance to American history but it did not view them necessarily as heritage patrimony. All of this changed with Horace Albright in the 1920s. He recognized the important role the federal government could play in the historic preservation movement.

However, Albright was not creating from whole cloth, though, when he maneuvered to position the NPS as a forceful historic preservation advocate.

When the NPS was founded in 1916, the enabling legislation stated that "historic conservation" would be a part of the new agency's responsibility.[198] The NPS also became responsible for administering the Antiquities Act of 1906, which had been administered by the Department of the Interior itself prior to the creation of the NPS as an agency within Interior.

Under Albright, "The federal government became a major force in the preservation picture."[199] During Albright's brief five-year tenure as director of the NPS, "The first three eastern historic sites had come into the Park System along with a crew of young historians who were to interpret these treasures to the visiting public."[200] This last point was crucial to the long-term development of the NPS. The development of the historic preservation field within the NPS required a dramatic influx of new, professional staff. The hiring of "archeologists, architects, and landscape architects [provided] a forum for professional debates on major issues in historic preservation."[201]

WANJ, as the new legislated partner to the Morristown Park, did continue to maintain two other patterns prevalent in the developing field of historic preservation. Members, still exclusively men at the time of the park's founding, were driven by patriotism, and they were nearly all quite wealthy. These two motives, patriotism and wealth, "became intertwined with educational motives in the mind of ...early proponents of the movement."[202] Until about 1950, this pattern of preservation would dominate the American approach to the topic. "Interest in [a] monument for the monument's sake, rather than for what happened at it" was not a generally accepted approach until the mid-twentieth century outside of the military realm.[203]

With Albright's vision, and the determination of Lloyd Smith and Clyde Potts, the NPS entered the rarified field of historic preservation at a time in America's history when the national mood was less than optimistic.

In the end, after the presidential signature, the NPS, Lloyd Smith and Clyde Potts could look back on the past few years and find solace in the fact that "the relatively smooth orchestration of the events leading up to the creation of the park...[was marked] with deep local support, impeccable timing, and clever maneuvers."[204]

1939

The mansion now had a new owner. Having aggressively positioned itself in the historic preservation field, the NPS was now responsible for the care and presentation of the mansion. It was not until 1938, however, that the NPS "began to plan for a change in the interpretation of the Ford Mansion."[205] From 1933 to 1938, the NPS seems to have spent most of its time on figuring out how to handle historic preservation before actually doing any major renovation work. The first recorded reference to renovation work on the mansion is 1935, when NPS "Deputy Chief Architect Charles Peterson set in motion the first concrete planning for work on the Mansion."[206] Part of the delay in restoration of the mansion was due to construction of the museum building.

The museum building, designed by noted Colonial Revival architect John Russell Pope in 1935, represented one of the first purposefully built museums in the NPS. Pope's museum and landscape were designed to complement the mansion and provide a place for the exhibition of the association's museum collections. WANJ maintained its collection in displays within the mansion that seemed ready to burst beyond the walls. The NPS had decided to provide a new venue for the collection before embarking on major renovation at the mansion, which promised to be more complicated.

To prepare plans for the renovation of the mansion, the NPS picked architect Thomas Waterman. Waterman was well known in the historic preservation movement, having worked on projects at Colonial Williamsburg and at the Henry Francis DuPont museum at Winterthur. Waterman and his assistant, Daniel Jensen, completed two reports in advance of restoration work at the mansion.

Although the association was a good steward of the mansion, by 1935 the structure was over 160 years old. It had for the past 60 years been utilized in ways for which it was not designed, and major work had been postponed for several decades. Alterations were necessary to open the mansion as a historically restored and furnished home rather than as a historic house filled with museum exhibits, as the association presented it.

The first item on the NPS renovation agenda was a new roof. Along with the roof went downspouts, gutters, shingles and the removal of the dormers. It was well known that the rear (north side) dormers were association-era additions. The front dormers predated the association, but it was not known by how much. Eventually, the NPS determined that the south-side dormers were also post-1780 (the Washington period). It was thus recommended "that all dormers on the building be removed in connection with the roof repairs on the basis that the buildings will...present a more accurate picture of its appearance during the period with which it is associated."[207] This memo is the first documented instance of the NPS proposing to return the mansion to its appearance during Washington's stay.

Ford Mansion from southwest, 1939. *Historic American Buildings Survey.*

Ford Mansion from the east, 1939. *Historic American Buildings Survey.*

The restoration plan was a large order. The plan called for

> *the replacement of all six-over-six sash with twelve-over-twelve, alterations to the fenestration in the wing, the replacement of all non-original hardware, the removal of plaster and exposure of beams in the wing, and the reconstruction of the Dutch oven.*[208]

Even with this large list, structural issues were not mentioned. The emphasis was on getting the appearance of the mansion correct. The mansion still suffered from rotten sills and framing members and a fractured foundation in the wing. To compound this, powder post beetles had infested the structure, and continued heavy visitation had badly damaged the infrastructure.[209]

With the restoration completed, the overall scheme for the preservation of the headquarters complex was also completed. The mansion now had the appearance, as best as could be determined in 1940, of the structure that Washington utilized. The two buildings allowed the NPS to more fully present the history and story of the mansion and of the Revolutionary period.

While the records of the first major renovation of the Ford Mansion in 1939 are sparse, the end goal—restoration to a 1779–80 appearance—is clear enough to ascertain. What is in question, however, is the methodological approach to the process that brought the mansion to the historical appearance desired.[210]

In 1937, chief architect Thomas Waterman sought to document architectural elements by categories determined by age. This was a difficult task given the lack of records from the Ford family and from the association. Waterman was forced to rely on his experience with old homes and his knowledge of building practices of the past 150 years. Fortunately, Waterman's expertise allowed him to generate a study that was reasonably accurate, and it allowed the NPS to move forward with restoration plans.[211]

In terms of outward appearance, the dormers and the windows throughout the mansion were the most obvious points of contention in the desire of the NPS to return the mansion to the period of significance. The north dormers were known to have been association additions, while the south dormers were of an earlier period. Waterman determined through examination of carpentry techniques that the south dormers could not have been earlier than 1830. Similarly, the six-over-six sash windows were known to be of a much later date than 1779–80. Colonial architecture was well known to have utilized a twelve-over-twelve sash design. The restoration of the roof and

Ford Mansion from southeast, 1939. *Historic American Buildings Survey.*

windows provided visitors the first glimpse in over one hundred years of the mansion as it looked in 1779–80.

Among other interior changes that Waterman pursued under the NPS was the changing of door opening positions, chair rail removal and additions, new plaster and floorboards and new hardware, along with many other subtle changes. The effect of the "makeover" was to create an atmosphere for visitors that re-created the time period that made the NPS interested in the Ford Mansion to begin with. Without the significance of the Washington connection, the Ford Mansion would not have had the national significance to warrant NPS involvement.

The last major restoration occurred in 1963 and incorporated elements of the newly discovered Ford family papers. Unfortunately, the papers did not contain much new information, although some changes were justified. Based in part on Gabriel's journals, the NPS removed sandstone steps and replaced them with wood. The door on the south side of the wing was centered, and shutters were removed from the second-story windows.

Celebrating the Ford Mansion and the National Park Service in 1972: Mrs. Mildred Ward and her cake, which treated five hundred. *Private collection.*

Dates of major restoration work by the NPS were 1939, 1948 and 1964. Throughout the 1970s and 1980s, most of the work was of a general maintenance nature with the exception of the replacement of the roof in 1986.

NEW DEAL PRESSURES

In addition to the Works Progress Administration presence, Morristown provided an excellent opportunity for the employment of a variety of New Deal programs. The Civilian Conservation Corps was an integral part of the success of the park in the beginning years. The CCC "participated in important restoration and reconstruction projects around the park, as well as archeological investigations."[212] The "CCC crews completed much of the Headquarters-museum landscape between 1936 and 1941 in accordance with the approved plans."[213] The NPS had brought Norman Newman onboard to work on designing the landscape for the new museum building in relation with the mansion. "His symmetrical design linked the museum to the mansion with an axial path that lead from [the] south entrance of the museum to the north entrance of the mansion, right on center."[214] The design that Newman envisioned combined elements of the Beaux Arts, European Renaissance and Colonial Revival styles to produce a striking mixture of formal and informal settings, which when combined acted to seamlessly connect the new museum building with the mansion. This connection left no doubt to visitors that the two buildings were to be approached as extensions of the same experience. In essence, the two buildings became one.

The future of Morristown National Historical Park no doubt lies partly in its past, but not exclusively the Revolutionary past. The final paragraph of the Integrated Cultural Resource study states:

> *The development of historic preservation in America began with an interest in the homes and lives of major historical figures, and in locations where pivotal events occurred in the formative days of the nation. Presently, a much wider spectrum of historic resources is of interest to members of the public, reflecting the agendas and interests of people of different backgrounds who have divergent perspectives on American history. While the Park was founded during an era of heightened interest in the Revolution and its major figures, the public may be best served in the future by a more general exploration of the social and economic development of the Morristown area. Fortunately, the Park contains a variety of cultural resources that will enable the analysis of this development not only during the Colonial period, but leading up to the present day.*[215]

The NPS in the twenty-first century has just as much of a challenge as the early NPS did in 1933. After more than seventy-five years as a national park, Morristown's goal remains much the same as it did when it first started in 1933. The park, however, has recognized that demographics change over time and acknowledges that new and innovative exhibits are necessary to engage a more sophisticated visitor.

Through all of this, the mansion still stands much as it did when Jacob Ford Jr. began building it in 1772. In 2012, the mansion will be 240 years old. Although it now relies on steel beams to help it remain upright under the weight of visitation, the mansion will no doubt continue to be a unique fixture on the Morristown landscape for many more years to come.

Afterword

History and Washington Reverence

Since at least the 1940s, the phrase "George Washington slept here" has had a comical, not altogether serious, meaning to it. The 1940 Moss Hart and George Kaufman play *George Washington Slept Here* was turned into a movie in 1942 starring Jack Benny and Ana Sheridan. The dilapidated farmhouse around which most of the story revolves is rumored to have been a place where Washington spent the night. The playwrights certainly did not invent this phrase or the somewhat mocking approach to the study of history that it implies. Moss Hart and George Kaufman were no doubt feeding off some larger response of in the general public toward this type of superficial approach to history. Perhaps it was somewhat related to the bicentennial of Washington's birth in 1932, when the owners of nearly every house that was located in the original thirteen colonies over two hundred years old felt compelled or obligated to find some Washington connection. The play's title also feeds off the public's perception that such statements could not have been completely true. In other words, could a person believe every historic house's claim to have hosted Washington?

The phrase has since become something of a humorous sideline to the more serious approach of a fuller understanding of the well-traveled General Washington during the American Revolutionary War. During eight years of war, Washington would have had to spend the night somewhere for 2,920 nights. Conceivably, there could be as many sites claiming that Washington spent the night as there were nights that required a place for him to billet. Whether Washington's presence adds luster to a

Washington slept here imagery (utilizing the famous painting by Emanuel Leutze of Washington crossing the Delaware) in contemporary use. *Morris County Tourism Bureau.*

historic site in the twenty-first century is an artificial way to view the many non-Washington contributions to American history of the structures that claim Washington's presence. The study of a historic site associated with Washington, though, can no doubt benefit from promoting that connection.

Saturday, October 7, 1995
Preview 8:00 A.M. - Auction 9:01 A.M.
FEATURING:
VICTORIAN BARBER CHAIR
(reported to have been used by George Washington!)

LOCATION: At the Jct. of Route 9 & 31, at the Corner Store, take Rt. 31 North, past the Pierce Homestead; go through Upper Village; then take Cooledge Road, approximately 2 miles, to our Auction Barn.

IN PART: Barber Chair, said to have been used to help cut George Washington's hair (note Aunt Emma sent w/Barber Chair--"1784 Washington visited at foot of Lake Otsego!!!"); 4-drawer Federal Bureau/walnut burl, graduated dovetail drawers & heavy chamfering; Ogee SETH THOMAS Mantle Clock; huge 6 board Blanket Chest; Cottage Commode and Bureaus; Mahogany and Oak Bureaus; square Oak Table w/extra leaves; round Maple Table w/4 matching Chairs; Tables, Stands; Salem Rocker and other Chairs; Antique 6' Drugstore Sign; Iron Kettles; nice Canadian Rag Blanket; Knickknacks & Flea Market Items; boxes of Piano/Organ Music; Andirons; Pintal Hinges; Pine Coffee Table; fancy Settee (rough); Rugs; Pictures & Picture Frames; Paintings; Baskets; Empire & other Mirrors; Costume Jewelry; Candle Holders; old Sleds and Snowshoes; Phonograph Records; Table Lamps; Crock; Milk Scale; Piano Bench (Victorian).

MODERN: Sofabed; Stuffed Chairs; 6' Sewing Table/SINGER Machine; Beds; Pots and Pans; Kitchenware; and lots and lots of everyday items.
AUCTIONEER'S NOTE: Two loads will be coming in on Sunday, too late to list.
TERMS: Cash or Good Check

Victorian barber chair—possibly used by George Washington? It would likely have been impossible for Washington to use a Victorian-style chair as he died decades before the style became fashionable. If it helps to sell, though, use it. *Morristown National Historical Park.*

Concerning the early twentieth century, "It is not too farfetched to say that there was a degree of competition among organizations claiming to have acquired a part of Washington—and the country's—history."[216] However, too many historic sites risk becoming nothing more than a "Washington slept here" site and consequently risk losing their historical relevance by becoming unwilling participants in a humorous sideline. Such historic sites become throwaway representations of historical dismissiveness and casualties of the trend to focus on one historic topic at the expense of all others. These significant historic sites risk suffering the fate of being reduced to the same level of understanding as the pervasive belief that Washington had wooden teeth.

While the Ford Mansion is indeed a site at which Washington slept, we must expand its history dramatically beyond the usual "Washington slept here" model. The presence of Washington cannot in any way be diminished or overlooked, but it represents only one period of the life of the structure. Washington's presence represents about six months out of the Ford Mansion's total history of over 235 years. The overwhelming history (in terms of time) of the structure is associated with periods of American history that are greatly removed from Washington in time and purpose.

What, then, is to be made of the Ford Mansion? How much of it can be said to be the genuine article in terms of historical significance, and how much is simply sentimental showmanship? Prior to the Civil War, it is estimated that at least four hundred books and articles on Washington were published.[217] "His image was revered as sacred, and many writers capitalized pronouns referring to him as is done with God in the Christian tradition."[218] Concerning the early days of the WANJ, "Like all curatorial activity, the WANJ's management of the Ford house and associated collections, could usefully be studied as a project of strategic planning and management of cultural resources, in a context of the nationwide development of patriotic historiography and curatorship.[219]

In particular, concerning Washington veneration, the story gets somewhat murky when trying to discern individual motives. Although there were vast announcements about saving the Ford Mansion for future generations, "It is not clear that there was ever an expectation that the 'lower orders' would visit the house."[220] Rather, it would seem that members joined in "an attempt…to affiliate their own identities with that of heroic national leaders and an unquestionably patriotic national past."[221]

The latter nineteenth century was a time of unprecedented growth, which not everyone agreed was a good thing. "A feeling that big money was devaluing the meaning of ancestry and education was what inspired many Anglo-Americans with pedigrees to join in efforts to save and treasure old colonial houses and their furnishings."[222] Yet many wealthy WANJ members were pursuing the business ethic that ancestor-venerating groups detested. How these groups came together for a common cause is an aspect of the Ford Mansion that awaits further study.

On one hand it may seem irrelevant to need to understand what it is that motivated people in the early 1870s to preserve the Ford Mansion or other historic houses. Of course, though, this misses the obvious question of how to justify one's existence if motivation is taken out of the equation. Knowing people's motives could be beneficial to the preservation movement overall if it could be determined what makes people want to preserve. A 1999 book, *Domesticating History*, is an attempt to understand the desires and aspirations of groups of preservationists over a roughly one-hundred-year period. It is part of the author's thesis that preservation of historic sites is as much a sociopolitical factor as it is commemoration. The publisher writes that *Domesticating* "shows how historic houses reflect less the lives and times of their famous inhabitants than the political pressures of the eras during which they were transformed into museums."[223]

APPENDIX 1

Gabriel Ford Physical Landscape Changes, 1805–1849

Year	Action	Source
1813	Planted the courtyard with potatoes	Massey 1975:7
1813	Improved 1780 stable with new sides, roof and addition	Massey 1975:7
ca. 1813	Filled the icehouse pit	Massey 1975:7
1814	Sowed courtyard with flax, clover, and timothy seed	Massey 1975:7
1814	Planted 2 larch trees	Massey 1975:6
1814	Maintained a parterre garden (mainly vegetable, but ornamentals too) to side or behind house, divided in quarters by a crosswalk and enclosed by a post and rail fence	Massey 1975:8
1814	Used manure and crop rotations to maintain soil	Massey 1975:8
1814	Used an artificially heated planting flat (hotbed) for plant propagation	Massey 1975:8
1814	Maintained a root cellar	Massey 1975:8
1814	Planted a Canadian dogwood, clithera [*Qethra*?], broom, and magnolia in the lowest garden square, west of die middle walk	Massey 1975:8
1815	Built a smokehouse	Massey 1975:7

1816	Painted die fence and outbuildings white	Massey 1975:8
1816	Planted several white pines and two horse chestnuts on the grounds	Massey 1975:6
1816	Planted rosyefsia, hibiscus, and sweet-scented shrubs in the garden	Massey 1975:8
1816	Ordered 8 horse chestnuts, 6 mountain ashes, 2 chestnuts, 4 beure pears, and 2 lindens from the Prince Nursery to plant along the courtyard border	Massey 1975:6
1816	Diagrammed a 3/8-acre lot bordered by pecan and pear cribs, a smokehouse, and a privy	Massey 1975:8
1817	Rebuilt icehouse to be 13 square feet	Massey 1975:8
1818	Reconfigured the 1790s fence	Massey 1975:7
1818	Planted 2 hawthorns	Massey 1975:7
1818	Transferred sheep from the courtyard to the road lot to maintain the turf	Massey 1975:7
1818	Spring house windmill destroyed by wind	Massey 1975:7
1819	Built a stone cistern in the courtyard near the southern kitchen door (stored 328 gallons of rainwater from roof)	Massey 1975:7
1819	Removed some of 1793 lombardy poplars	Massey 1975:7
1819	Scythe was used for mowing the turf	Massey 1975:7
1819	Lawn was fertilized with manure	Massey 1975:7
1820	"Headed down" and removed many of the remaining Lombardy poplars	Massey 1975:7
1822	Planted 2 hawthorns on the grounds and 3 in the garden	Massey 1975:7
1822	Designated garden parterres as east and west squares, each being % square acre (ca. 10,890 square feet or 104 by 104 foot)	Massey 1975:8
1823	1819 cistern collapsed and was rebuilt	Massey 1975:7
1823	Planted a lilac border and 10 black locusts on the grounds	Massey 1975:8

Gabriel Ford Physical Landscape Changes, 1805–1849

1823	Planted a horse chestnut and paper mulberry scions in the garden	Massey 1975:8
1823	Planted purple jasmine scions by front and back doors of hall	Massey 1975:8
1824	Planted a white thorn on the grounds	Massey 1975:7
1824	Planted grapevines on the mounds left by the poplars in the courtyard	Massey 1975:7
1824	Planted weeping willows in the gangway just outside the courtyard	Massey 1975:7
1825	Began hiring an annual gardener	Massey 1975:9
1825	Purchased a hotbed frame with hinged wooden covers	Massey 1975:9
1825	Planted sweet-scented shrubs and flowering almonds under the front windows of the house	Massey 1975:8
1826	Planted multiflora roses, one under each window of the drawing and dining rooms	Massey 1975:8
1835	Built a milkhouse	Massey 1975:8
1835	Established a plant nursery behind the woodhouse	Massey 1975:8
1836	Maintained a 10 by 19 foot shed	Massey 1975:9
1840	Built a root cellar in die garden	Massey 1975:9
1840	Diagrammed the garden squares, and the size had not changed since the 1820s	Massey 1975:9

Source: Taken from the "Cultural Landscape Report for Washington's Headquarters."

APPENDIX 2

Henry A. Ford's Physical Landscape Changes, 1849–1873

YEAR	ACTION	SOURCE
1856	Ordered garden seed from Hosack including lima bean and sweet corn seed	Massey 1975:9
1858	Planted West Indian parsnip	Massey 1975:9
1859	Planted onion, lima bean, bell pepper, watermelon, sweet Mexican corn, okra, tomato, salif, squash, muskmelon, cabbage, sweet corn, parsnips, beets, eggplant, naturion [*Nasturtium*?], raspberry, and grape seeds or plants	Massey 1975:9
1859	Planted two maple trees in the courtyard, one replaced a dead horse chestnut near the house	Massey 1975:9
1860	Subdivided the southwestern portion of the Ford property for building lots	Bertland 1981:29
1861	Maintained ornamental shrubs and trees in front of the house	Hughes 1861
1863	Installed a "hydraulic ram" (water pump) to deliver water to kitchen for storage (neglected the cistern)	Massey 1975:10
1872	Will mentions "the old garden spot with fruit, the Pomarium and Lawn in front to the middle of Morris Street"	Jacobs 1993: 37

Source: Taken from the "Cultural Landscape Report for Washington's Headquarters."

APPENDIX 3

Fire Insurance Application of Henry A. Ford

Application of Henry A. Ford of the township of Morris, county of Morris New Jersey to the Rahway Mutual Fire Insurance Company for Insurance against loss by Fire for the term of __ years, for the sum of Three Thousand Dollars on the following property, to wit, on his double two story Dwelling house, Kitchen & Shed or Leanto in Morristown, hereinafter more particularly described.

Estimated value	$12000 [18,000?]
Amount proposed for Insurance	3000
Amount of Premium Note	240
Amount of Cash	30.

Said Dwelling House &c is situated in Morristown N. Jersey, about three quarters of a mile from the Morris Green, near the junction of the Turnpike Road leading to Elizabeth Town & the road leading to Whippany and is commonly called "Washington's Headquarters" late the residence of the Honl. Gabriel H. Ford deceased, now owned & occupied by Applicant, as his family Residence.

The Buildings are principally of wood, though generally filled in with Brick, except the Shed or Leanto & are in good tenantable condition having been lately about the year 1853, thoroughly repaired & painted outside & in &c.

The size of the main building is about fifty four feet front, by about thirty two feet deep, two stories high, with good cellar underneath the whole [and] Garret above, not finished off. A wide Hall through on the lower or first floor, on which are four rooms, two on each side of the Hall, with stair way, leading to the Second Story. On the Second Story [p. 2] floor there are five bed rooms, besides a Hall common to them, & from which there is a closet [closed?] stair way to the Garret above the whole.

The Kitchen or Wing is also two stories high but not of the height of the Main building & is about thirty two feet in front by about twenty seven feet deep. On the lower floor is a Hall or Rutder [?] from front to rear, the Main Kitchen Room and two small apartments,—one used Ordinarily as a store room & the other as a pantry. There is a stair way leading from the entry & taken off of it to the Second Story, on which are five bed rooms besides passages, from one of which is a stair way to the Garret above which is unfinished. By this Stair way there is also a communication with the back room of the Main building giving access to & from the Main building & Wing. There is also a passage way from the Kitchen below to the Leanto & from this passageway a narrow stair way to one of the back bedrooms above.

The Shed or Leanto is in rear of the Kitchen & is about nineteen feet long by about ten feet wide.

There are two chimneys to the Main building and one to the Wing or Kitchen. In the Main building there were originally seven fireplaces, but these have been closed up with Brick &c., with Stove pipe aperture at each except one (the parlor) in which there is a Coal Grate. It being the intention to use (optionally) at each of the others, stoves for wood or coal, and a stove for wood or coal in the back room on the first floor of the Main building, used occasionally [p. 3] as a Bedroom and Library & Office. There is a large Range & [?] stove for coal or wood in the principal Hall, with pipe passing through the Ceiling, guardedly to the Hall above into a Drum there & from there [?] through a partition also guardedly into one of the back rooms where it, where it [sic] communicates Carefully with the Stack of the chimney.

There is a Cooking range in the Kitchen with an Oven attached, beside a Common brick oven underneath which is a safe place for wood ash [bin?] & in the Kitchen are the Water arrangements of Copper Boiler &c.

Fire Insurance Application of Henry A. Ford

All the buildings are covered with Shingles & there are lightning rods terminating at each of the Chimneys.

There were two Stone cisterns formerly in use near the Kitchen door for rain water, but these have been in a measure neglected & one out of use, the premises being supplied with spring water [from a distance?] by means of a Hydraulic Ram which sends a supply into a large Tank holding many barrels in the Kitchen Garret from which it is carried to a Bath room below laden off of one of the Kitchen bed rooms & thereto in the Kitchen to the Kitchen fixtures & improvements below.

This application and term being some but not very essentially for [from?] my written application to the Company on or about the 24. Decr. 1853, and from my after Statement written to the Company on or about the 26. March 1860 [?], to both of which I here refer.

There is Insurance of the premises with Newark Mutual Fire Association Company of Two thousand Eight [p. 4] hundred dollars ($2800.) Policy ending 23d Septemr. 1863. Also in the Bergen County Farmers Mutual Fire Insurance Company for Two Hundred Dollars ($200). Policy ending March 2nd 1865.

Henry A. Ford
Applicant

Source: Morristown National Historical Park Library; Ford Family Papers, 1738/9–1904; Book 9, Series II; Box 4, Folder 2.

APPENDIX 4

Washington's Headquarters at Morristown, New Jersey

Come hither, little grandson mine, and sit upon
my knee,
I'll tell thee a tale of olden days, a tale of chivalry,
I'll tell thee of the noble men—one nobler than
them all—
Who dwelt beneath this old rooftree and walked
this very hall.

Look well about you, boy, look well, for 'tis not
every day
In these fast times they chance to let a house like
this one stay;
I heard that some would pull it down, but men
were found at last
To keep the old house standing as a memory of
the past.

Beneath this grand old rooftree, boy, your country's father came
To fight the fight which gave to you that country
and a name;
And to him gathered all the brave, a small but
gallant band,
Who dared to ask that Liberty should reign
throughout the land

Here, when the days were darkest and the strug-
-gle seemed in vain,
The patriot chieftain fought the fight and won
immortal fame
Not thirty miles across the Reds were camped in
Great array,
While here was but a feeble band to block their
bloody way.

Look off on yonder hillside, boy, 'tis scarce a
mile away
'Tis there the patriot army though the bitter
Winter lay;
A trilling walk it seems to-day but then, on snow
and sleet,
The path was marked with blood-stains from the
sentries' shoeless feet

In hunger oft, in sickness shore, with garments
thin and few
Both men and chieftain fared alike that bitter
Winter through;
And many a noble patriot died, as yon church-
yard can tell,
As also many afield and wood—just buried
where they fell.

But think, my boy, how oft "the man" has paced
this ample hall
And mused on danger, famine, plague, God
knows he met them all;
The long, long nights when other slept he
walked this floor,
It seems to echo back his tread as oft it did of
yore.

Washington's Headquarters at Morristown, New Jersey

The very walls seem whispering, in murmurs
soft and low,
And strive to tell their story of a hundred years
ago;
The stout old rafters gently creak as if they fain
would say
"We sheltered glorious Washington, beneath
our arms he lay."

May vandal's axe be never raised against the
Old rooftree
But tender hands keept upright still this refuge
of the free;
And when the times comes round, my boy, the
tale your sons to tell,
God grant, old house, you still may stand, and
till then fare you well.

D.A.W.

A Note on Sources

Throughout this book, inference has been used to describe the particular actions under discussion or to expand upon a particular theme regarding the Ford family or the Ford Mansion. The Ford Mansion is one of those unfortunate historic sites that have come to be defined largely with only one moment in history. Consequently, not much documentary evidence exists for the other periods of the mansion's story. Some of this is by design, but mostly it was due to negligence and happenstance. Therefore, it is necessary to extrapolate from similar sources what would most likely have been the case concerning the Ford Mansion. [224]

This is not an unusual device, as historical documentation is not equally distributed among the endless array of potential historical topics of study. One of the more famous examples of this was the biography of Ronald Reagan written by Richard Morris. Because of a lack of documentary evidence detailing the president's early life, biographer Morris invented a fictional character based on an "everyman" model of the time period and thus told Reagan's undocumented story through this surrogate. In a similar way, then, using someone like William Corbit, for whom mounds of documentation exist, to elucidate the Ford mansion story is appropriate. This process allows the Jacob Ford story to be told as an aggregate story, free from undue speculation. I feel this is both a reasonable and responsible reaction to the lack of primary documentation.

Twenty-six years ago, in 1983, on the fiftieth anniversary of the park, an attempt was made to compile a list of the most glaring outstanding historical questions left unanswered after having existed fifty years as a park.

It is much more important to be curious about what you do not know than to be comfortable with what you do know. Historical research and writing is all about building on the work that preceded your own. And it is about preparing the way for future generation of researchers, too. Therefore, having access to the broadest range of sources is critical. Conversely, having an awareness of what will not be found in a given range of sources is crucial, not only to know what to possibly look for, but also to know what to look for elsewhere in terms of similarity of purpose.

The ten most crucial unanswered questions in 1983 were:

1. *What are the actual dates of construction of the mansion?*
2. *By whom was it constructed?*
3. *What materials and techniques were used in construction?*
4. *What is the amount of original fabric remaining?*
5. *What changes have been made and what are their dates?*
6. *Is there a separate date for the construction of the kitchen?*
7. *Was there a different location for the kitchen?*
8. *Was there a different configuration for the main stairs?*
9. *How did any other stairway function in the mansion?*
10. *Was there a separate door in the room believed to have been used by Washington as his office?*

In terms of answering these questions, though, by researching the park files and archives, as well as the local public libraries, the document by Robert P. Guter concludes that "documentary descriptions [of the Ford mansion] have always amounted to little more than passing references"[225]—therefore relegating any detailed description on the building or utilization of the mansion as so far nonexistent.

The most likely source of information would most probably come from Jacob Ford Jr. "Considering Ford's socio-economic position and the high-style nature of the house he had built, it seems possible, even likely, that he participated to some degree in its design," but no type of Ford documentation relating to this topic exists.[226] Whether documentation ever existed is unknown. The known facts make the unknown so much more glaring. A journal or diary by Jacob Ford Jr. would probably prove to be one of the most important finds should it ever happen to surface and assuming he kept one. It is entirely possible that Ford did not see the need to keep detailed records. He may not have had an inclination to write. Mrs. Ford may have purposely, or accidentally, destroyed her husband's letters and journals. "In short, no useful sources from the earliest period of the house are known to exist."[227] The best that can be hoped for are "chance discoveries."[228] While this is a bleak assessment of the remaining documentation concerning the Ford mansion's early years, it should in no way deter from the future work of historians to further increase our understanding of the American past.

In addition to the paucity of original sources pertaining to the Ford Mansion and the Morristown encampment overall, it is recommended in at least one major study of the park to move beyond the familiar confines of the Washington story and concentrate on other aspects of what the park has to offer.[229] In particular, four areas are noted: one, industrial rural economy; two, agricultural rural economy; three, Native American settlement; and four, the country estate economy that developed near the Jockey Hollow area about 1900. The Integrated Cultural Resource Report summarizes its suggestions as follows:

> *It is recommended that all four contexts be used in the interpretation of the Park. While the encampments of the Revolutionary War were probably the most momentous historical events occurring within the Park's boundaries, Native American activities; the industrial processing of timber, iron, mica, lime, etc.; and agricultural/horticultural pursuits took place over a longer period. The era of the country place also had an important impact within the Park. These contexts are historically interesting.*

It should also be pointed out that many of the sources available and cited in the bibliography are at times mutually contradictory. Therefore, it is rather easy in some instances for someone reading this book to say "That is wrong" or "That fact is misrepresented." This is pointed out not to assuage criticism—on the contrary, it is invited; rather the point is made in an effort to make the reader aware that not everything that is in print is 100 percent accurate. The author has made every effort to determine facts when sources are at variance. Therefore, before alerting the author or publisher to a perceived error, ensure that all known sources are consulted.

Having made that disclaimer, the author recognizes and acknowledges that he alone is responsible for any genuine errors that may be a part of this book.

Notes

Chapter 1

1. From Henry Wadsworth Longfellow's poem "Haunted Houses," found at www.poets.org, Academy of American Poets. Naturally, this quote is not to imply that the Ford Mansion is haunted in the colloquial sense of the word. Rather, as Longfellow intended it, "haunted" implies that the mansion, or any old house, is never fully removed from the inhabitants who have occupied its space. As this book looks at the mansion over the course of 235 years, it is only natural that the mansion has compiled layers of history, and the story must be told as such. The mansion has accumulated the sense of many, many different people. The idea of haunted, then, is more like an approach to the concept of layered history. There are layers of occupation, of history, that are never erased. Therefore, a historic house never stops being what it was when it was originally built. And it can never stop being "haunted."
2. Richard L. Bushman, *The Refinement of America: Persons, Houses, Cities* (New York: Alfred A. Knopf, 1992), 132. "By the eighteenth century, the meaning of gentry houses so far exceeded the practical functions they performed as sheltered warm places for sleeping, eating, and work that houses became a form of literature. The houses were stage sets for dramas, and like the characters themselves, could be envisioned within the frame of a story." Mansions, therefore, cease to be practical places and move into the realm of showplace. They become a dynamic space in which events great and small (where all the events are important) are

performed. Bushman continues: "Nothing deserved portraiture until it had a part in some societal myth, and placing a picture of a house within a frame was like putting a story within the covers of a book." The museum collection at Morristown contains over one hundred images of the mansion. This could mean then that the mansion has attained the level of societal myth.

3. A report dated November 2, 1875, shows that the Washington Association had to deal with considerable structural and cosmetic challenges. In one section, the report stated: "In the interior very considerable alterations were obliged to be made, especially in the second story, where an entire room had to be taken away to restore the hall to its original proportions. The walls, ceiling and fireplaces were so dilapidated that it was found necessary to renew the greater part of them. On the main floor much remains to be done in repairing walls and ceilings." Taken from Judith M. Jacob, "Historic Structure Report," part I, "Ford Mansion," Morristown National Historical Park, NPS, draft, October 1993, Architectural Data Washington Association, 1–2.
4. Jacob, "Historic Structure Report," part I, "Ford Mansion," 1–2.

Chapter 2

5. Ibid., Historical Data Ford Family, 1. The family can be traced to Weymouth, Massachusetts, in the mid-seventeenth century. The family was of purely English origin and worked their way southward through New England during the closing years of the seventeenth century before settling in northern New Jersey by 1710.
6. "Morristown National Historic Park Cultural Landscape Report for Washington's Headquarters," (Boston, MA: National Park Service, Olmsted Center for Landscape Preservation, 2005), 15.
7. Ibid., 13.
8. Ibid., 14.
9. Theodore Thayer, *Colonial and Revolutionary Morris County* (Morristown: Morris County Heritage Commission, 1975), 90–91.
10. The Colony of New Jersey was originally divided between West and East Jersey. West Jersey was the generally barren part of the state and had little population. East Jersey was considered very productive and had a vibrant population. During the Revolution, New Jersey officially became one.
11. Thayer, *Colonial and Revolutionary*, 34.

12. "Cultural Landscape Report," 13–14.
13. Thayer, *Colonial and Revolutionary*, 33.
14. Ibid., 34.
15. Vera B. Craig, and Ralph H. Lewis, "Furnishing Plan for the Ford Mansion (1779–1780)," Morristown National Historical Park, 1976, 22.
16. William U. Massey, "Historical Grounds Survey of Washington's Headquarters, Ford Mansion," Morristown, NJ: May 1975, 4.
17. "Integrated Cultural Resource Report: Morristown National Historical Park," draft (Amherst: University of Massachusetts Archeological Services, 2001), 57.
18. Peter O. Wacker, *The Cultural Geography of Eighteenth Century New Jersey* (Trenton: New Jersey Historical Commission, 1975), 6. Wacker continues: "Although Pennsylvania is often thought to have been the most heterogeneous colony in terms of the origins of her settlers, the title rightfully belongs to New Jersey, which began to be settled by large numbers of people of European origin well before the Penn colony was founded. New Jersey's ethnic and cultural diversity stemmed largely from two factors—her geographical position and her political history."
19. John T. Cunningham, *New Jersey: America's Main Road* (Garden City: Doubleday & Company, Inc., 1966), 51.
20. "Integrated Cultural Resource Report," 57.
21. A short pamphlet published in 1683 by the Scots Proprietors, presumably for consumption in Scotland, began its account of East New Jersey by stating, "It is a Matter beyond all Question, that Plantations in *America*, is a thing of a great Advantage to the Nations of Europe." Included in the pamphlet is the patent from King Charles II to his brother the Duke of York. Part of the patent lists six Scotsman who as proprietors had responsibility for the area that today is northern New Jersey. The patent goes on to describe the physical characteristics of the area, the environment, etc. The copy was originally published in the *Historical Magazine* in 1865. Private reprint of copied article, Morrisania, New York, 1867.
22. Cunningham, *New Jersey*, 51. The paragraph continues, "The two areas took on definite 'tone': West Jersey becoming closely identified with the philosophy of the mild Quakers, East Jersey with the more militant Presbyterians. West Jersey became an area of large farms and plantations, as the result of both land policies and fewer colonists, while East Jersey assumed a pattern of power concentrated in town governments jealous of their local prerogatives."

23. Wacker, *Cultural Geography*, 14.
24. Thayer, *Colonial and Revolutionary*, 13. By 1714, they had purchased much of the land that would later become Morristown.
25. Dennis P. Ryan, "Six Towns: Continuity and Change in Revolutionary New Jersey, 1770–1792," PhD diss., New York University, 1974, 7. Further: "The cultural, ethnic, and religious diversity of East Jersey is the prominent fact in any analysis of the region's early history. East Jersey was by far the most heterogeneous area in the most diverse colony, and a precursor of future American migration patterns." Dennis P. Ryan, "Six Towns: Continuity and Change in Revolutionary New Jersey, 1770–1792," PhD diss., New York University, 1974, 14.
26. "Cultural Landscape Report," 12.
27. Thayer, *Colonial and Revolutionary*, 55.
28. "Cultural Landscape Report," 14.
29. Thayer, *Colonial and Revolutionary*, 55.
30. Ibid., 65.
31. Ibid., 56.
32. "Integrated Cultural Resource Report," 69.
33. Ibid.
34. Ibid.
35. Larry R. Gerlach, *The Road to Revolution* (Trenton: New Jersey Historical Commission, 1975), 3.
36. Ibid., 9.
37. Ibid., 10.
38. Ibid., 13.
39. Thayer, *Colonial and Revolutionary*, 41.
40. Jacob, "Historic Structure Report," part I, "Ford Mansion," 5.
41. The earliest documented references to the mansion date to 1777, when Captain Rodney's Delaware troops were billeted in the Ford house. Rodney wrote that the mansion was "an Elegant one…having 4 rooms on a floor and two stories high." It is recorded to have been painted white, and in 1846 "it was described as being brick, covered with wood, and painted white." The most complete description of the house dates from the early 1860s, when Henry A. Ford, the builder's grandson, took out an insurance policy on the structure. He described it as a "double two story dwelling house [with] Kitchen & Shed or Lean to…principally of wood, though generally filled in with brick." All observations are quoted in Francis R. Holland Jr., "Historic Structure Report," part I, "Ford Mansion" (Morristown, NJ: Morristown National Historical Park, 1959), 6–7.

42. Jacob, "Historic Structure Report," part I, "Ford Mansion," 2.
43. "Cultural Landscape Report," 15.
44. In more formal architectural language, architect Thomas T. Waterman wrote: "The architectural ancestry of the Ford Mansion can be traced directly in the first of the High Renaissance house of England, Coleshill in Barkshire…built in 1640…the style came to this country probably first in the design of the Governor's Palace in Williamsburg, Virginia, started in 1705. This type became the familiar one for the mansion of the 18th century in all the Colonies. The style is characterized in the finer examples by a symmetrical façade, strong horizontal lines, produced by a heavy rich cornice (and in addition in the Ford Mansion by the belt cornice at the line of the second floor, a relatively rare feature in a frame building) and by the hipped roof. On account of the great depth of this house, the roof becomes a hip on a hip…The huge square chimney stacks are…characteristic [and] each serves four rooms." Quoted from Waterman's "The Architecture of the Ford Mansion" in Holland Jr., "Historic Structure Report," 1959, 12.
45. Bushman, *Refinement of America*, 101.
46. David Arbogast, "Inventory of Structures," Morristown National Historical Park, Cultural Resources Management Study No. 14, 1985, 279. During the nineteenth century, the Ford family replaced their aged colonial windows with more stylish six over six in the main part of the mansion. These Victorian-style windows remained on the mansion through the Washington Association period and were replaced by the Park Service in the 1930s.
47. Ibid.
48. The Jacob Ford Sr. House in Mount Hope, New Jersey, has much more of a large farmhouse feel and look to it. While massive, it lacks any architectural distinction. It could, however, have been a source of inspiration for the floor plan for the Morristown mansion as the two are nearly identical.
49. The issue of the main stairs at the Ford mansion has perplexed architectural historians for decades. There are only two confirmed absolutes. One is that the stairs currently used by visitors are not original to 1774. The original stairway did not have a switchback at the halfway point. The second absolute is that the original mansion did not have the same type of grand stairway as other mansions of the period—the original stairway was from the standpoint of size much like the one seen today and in the same location. Therefore, the discussion in this book concerning the stairs

is accurate in terms of the type and style of stairs that the Fords installed in their mansion. The question of where the stairs were originally located may or may not be determined. What can be ascertained is the social function of the installation of a smaller stairway and the aspect of this decision in terms of how the Fords saw their mansion and how they wanted it to be seen. The main outlines of the controversy are noted by Craig and Lewis: "When the Park Service undertook to restore the Ford House, the main stairs ran steeply in a single flight. The landing at the head of the stairs opened at the right into the main hall and at the left into the northwest room. The stairs themselves were impractical for visitor use and in the restoration architect's considered judgment [they were] not original." An earlier report states that until 1939 "physical evidence indicated that…they [the stairs] remained in their original location." Taken from George L. Wrenn, "Historic Structure Report," part II, "Architectural Data Section on the Ford Mansion" (Morristown, NJ: Morristown National Historical Park, 1963), 9. To add to the confusion, these two documents seem to be at variance. In 1939, Melvin Weig of Morristown NHP wrote: "The present restored stair was designed to fit the original framing. Unfortunately, no evidence came to light, either from physical or documentary sources, as to its exact form. However, the design has been kept as simple as possible, conformable to the requirements of space and local Colonial precedent for the balusters and trim." Taken from Jacob, "Historic Structure Report," part I, "Ford Mansion," 11.

50. Jacob, "Historic Structure Report," part I, "Ford Mansion," 11.
51. Bushman, *Refinement of America*, 120.
52. Without a grand staircase, "The rituals focusing on it, with all their subtle and not so subtle intimations of power, could also be eliminated, leaving guests free to experience the house and its pleasures as equals." Taken from Robert F. Dalzell Jr., and Lee Baldwin Dalzell, *George Washington's Mount Vernon: At Home in Revolutionary America* (New York: Oxford University Press, 1998), 96.
53. Bushman, *Refinement of America*, 119.
54. It is known circumstantially that Mrs. Ford did not seem to be on intimate terms with the wealthier citizens of the area who visited Washington during his stay. This could be because by the time of Washington's stay she was a widow and perhaps reluctant to socialize too much. However, it could also be that her actions reflect unfamiliarity with high society in the area. Taken from Craig & Lewis, "Furnishing Plan," 1976, 22.
55. Thayer, *Colonial and Revolutionary*, 80.

56. Bushman, *Refinement of America*, 103.
57. Steven M. Pulinka, *Discover the Historic Houses of Odessa* (Winterthur, DE: Henry Francis du Pont Winterthur Museum, 1999), 20.
58. Bushman, *Refinement of America*, 135. Bushman further states on 129 that "the installation of gardens [at mansions] became standard" after 1725.
59. "Cultural Landscape Report," 5.
60. One of the most reasonable explanations, although unproven, is that Jacob Ford Jr. became too involved with political and military affairs before the mansion could be fully designed and built. Taken from Massey, "Historical Grounds Survey," 3.
61. "Cultural Landscape Report," 15.
62. John A.H. Sweeney, *Grandeur on the Appoquinimink: The House of William Corbit at Odessa, Delaware* (Newark: University of Delaware Press, 1989), 69.
63. Bushman, *Refinement of America*, 113.
64. Thomas J. Archdeacon, *New Jersey Society in the Revolutionary Era* (Trenton: New Jersey Historical Commission, 1975), 29. Archdeacon writes: "In its essence, the American Revolution does not seem to have been caused by domestic issues, but economic and social factors were definitely among the myriad considerations which could affect an individual's reaction to it. Among the political elite, persons who had enjoyed great success under the empire were the most likely to value the old order, while leaders with primarily local ties were more aware of the opportunities offered by independence. These divergent patterns of response ultimately had important social consequences."
65. Ryan, "Six Towns," 13. Although the Revolution would dramatically change the lives of the colonists, "The people of East Jersey…all entered a new era in 1776, bringing with them a heritage of attitudes and institutions from the colonial past."
66. Larry R. Gerlach, ed, *New Jersey in the American Revolution 1763–1783: A Documentary History* (Trenton: New Jersey Historical Commission, 1975), 232.
67. *South Carolina Historical Magazine* XIII, no. 3 (July 1912): 132.
68. Howard Zinn, *A People's History of the United States* (New York: HarperPerennial, 1980), 109.
69. *South Carolina Historical Magazine* XIII, no. 3 (July 1912): 132. Timothy Ford recounts a story in his will concerning the sword his father carried during the Revolution. In indicating the importance of the sword he was bequeathing, he wrote, "My father's Revolutionary sword is in my

possession, after his death my beloved mother girded it on my thigh at the age of sixteen and I wore it in the field of Battle."

70. *South Carolina Historical Magazine* XIII, no. 3 (July 1912): 133.
71. Robert P. Guter, "Historical Data Investigation: The Jacob Ford Jr. Mansion, Washington's Headquarters." Prepared for the Morristown National Historical Park, Morristown, New Jersey, July 1983. CRBIB #012351, 15.
72. Ford Family papers. Morristown National Historical Park Archives.
73. Ibid.

CHAPTER 3

74. Dennis P. Ryan, *New Jersey's Loyalists* (Trenton: New Jersey Historical Commission, 1975), 8.
75. Cunningham, *New Jersey*, 62.
76. Ibid.
77. Zinn, *A People's History*, 62.
78. Ryan, "Six Towns," 111.
79. Ibid., 109.
80. Ibid., 112.
81. Gerlach, *Road to Revolution*, 12.
82. Cunningham, *New Jersey*, 68.
83. Ibid.
84. "Cultural Landscape Report," 19.
85. Ryan, "Six Towns," 124.
86. Ibid. Benjamin White commented, "We were so near the line, that in the fore part of the night we had British and Refugees, in the morning the American Troops." Found in Ryan, "Six Towns," 131.
87. Morristown National Historical Park Archives, microfilm reel 44: 196–98.
88. Zinn, *A People's History*, 76.
89. "Cultural Landscape Report," 21. See also Gerlach, *New Jersey*, 4.
90. Gerlach, *Road to Revolution*, 2.
91. Ibid. Gerlach continues: "Ranking ninth in population…and tenth in territory…among the twelve mainland colonies and…possessing little commercial manufacturing and scant direct import-export trade with Europe and other American provinces, and boasting no special cash crop…New Jersey had little influence on inter-colonial or imperial affairs."

92. Gerlach, *New Jersey*, 231. Dennis P. Ryan writes: "The Loyalists of New Jersey came from all classes of society. While some enjoyed an economy significantly above that of the majority of the population, there were also many poor and marginal individuals who served in Loyalist brigades, so that it would not be accurate to classify the friend of Britain as an elite aristocrat." Found in Ryan, *New Jersey's Loyalists*, 11.
93. Thayer, *Colonial and Revolutionary*, 130.
94. Ibid.
95. Ryan, "Six Towns," 117.
96. Thayer, *Colonial and Revolutionary*, 37.
97. John Fiske, *The American Revolution* (Boston: Houghton, Mifflin and Company, n.d.), 130.
98. Thayer, *Colonial and Revolutionary*, 123.
99. Gerlach, *Road to Revolution*, 26.
100. "The Revolution plunged the states of Delaware, Maryland, North Carolina, South Carolina, Georgia, and, to a much lesser degree, Virginia, into divisive civil conflicts that persisted during the entire period of struggle." Ronald Hoffman as quoted in Zinn, *A People's History*, 81.
101. Gerlach, *Road to Revolution*, 9.
102. Ibid.
103. Gerlach, *New Jersey*, 76.
104. Zinn, *A People's History*, 83. Zinn is quoting Edmund Morgan.
105. Ryan, "Six Towns," 126.
106. Gerlach, *Road to Revolution*, 14.
107. Gerlach, *New Jersey*, 231.
108. Ibid., 232.
109. Ryan, *New Jersey's Loyalists*, 12.
110. Zinn, *A People's History*, 76.
111. Ibid.
112. Gerlach, *New Jersey*, 231.
113. Ryan, *New Jersey's Loyalists*, 5.
114. Thayer, *Colonial and Revolutionary*, 130.
115. Zinn, *A People's History*, 76. See also Gerlach, *New Jersey*, 28.
116. Gerlach, *New Jersey*, 233.
117. Ibid.
118. Ibid.
119. "Integrated Cultural Resource Report," 69.
120. Ibid., 70.
121. "Cultural Landscape Report," 20.

122. Ibid.
123. Jacob, "Historic Structure Report," part I, "Ford Mansion," 10.
124. http://memory.loc.gov/cgi-bin/query/P?mgw:1:./temp/~ammem_pWpj::@@@mdb=rbpebib,coolbib,mtj,scsmbib,mal,mjm,mcc,papr,pin,presp,mgw,nfor.
125. Ibid.
126. Ibid.
127. Ibid.

Chapter 4

128. Jacob, "Historic Structure Report," part I, "Ford Mansion," 4.
129. "Integrated Cultural Resource Report," 27.
130. Ibid., 32. See appendices 1 and 2 for a complete list of the documented changes of Gabriel Ford and his son Henry Ford during the periods of their ownership of the property. The chart in appendix 1 represents the most complete list of documented work at the estate. By far, Gabriel was the one Ford who altered the landscape most and the one who kept the most detailed account of his accounts.
131. Ibid., 32.
132. Ibid.
133. Ibid.
134. Ibid., 33.
135. Ibid., 34.
136. Cunningham, *New Jersey*, 142.
137. "Integrated Cultural Resource Report," 26. The English traveler is John Melish.
138. Ibid.
139. Jacob, "Historic Structure Report," part I, "Ford Mansion," 15.
140. "Cultural Landscape Report," 18.
141. Cunningham, *New Jersey*, 153.
142. "Integrated Cultural Resource Report," 58.
143. Ibid., 29.
144. Cunningham, *New Jersey*, 131.
145. Ibid.
146. "Integrated Cultural Resource Report," 29.
147. Cunningham, *New Jersey*, 136.
148. Ibid., 139.

149. This is usually one of the indicators of the stability of a society. When families can transfer property from one generation to the next, the long-term viability of a social network is considerably strengthened.
150. "Cultural Landscape Report," 24.
151. Karal Ann Marling, *George Washington Slept Here: Colonial Revivals and American Culture, 1876–1986* (Cambridge, MA: Harvard University Press, 1988), 74.
152. Jacob, "Historic Structure Report," part I, "Ford Mansion," 1.
153. Ibid., 3. The article states: "And it is this classical locality, and this venerable mansion thick clustering with revolutionary reminiscences, which is to come under the common-place hammer of the auctioneer on the 25th of June. We do not look upon that event with pleasure. It seems a desecration, almost a sacrilege. The decadence of the Republic may date from the time when as Americans we begin to make merchandise of our sacred places, and jest with names of the departed great. The house in which Shakespeare was born is venerated by the entire civilized world, yet Shakespeare but gave us a book while Washington gave a country to unborn millions. A letter with his signature will bring a large sum, sold anywhere in Europe, yet we stand idly and curiously by, while the most sacred mementoes of him and of the Republic are scattered among a crowd of purchasers, moved by the voice of the auctioneer than by the sentiments of patriotism and respect."
154. Ibid., 4.
155. "Cultural Landscape Report," 25.
156. Laurel A. Racine, "Historic Furnishings Assessment," Morristown National Historical Park (Morristown, NJ: Northeast Museum Services Center, December 2003), 11.
157. "Cultural Landscape Report," 25.
158. "Integrated Cultural Resource Report," 84.

Chapter 5

159. Jacob, "Historic Structure Report," part I, "Ford Mansion," 6.
160. Ibid.
161. Ibid., 7.
162 "Cultural Landscape Report," 25.
163. "Integrated Cultural Resource Report," 80.

164. Ibid., 81.
165. Jacob, "Historic Structure Report," part I, "Ford Mansion," 5.
166. Ibid., 8.
167. Ibid.
168. Ibid.
169. Ibid., 9.
170. Ibid.
171. "Cultural Landscape Report," 50.
172. Ibid., 51.
173. Ibid., 51.
174. Marling, *George Washington Slept Here*, 74.
175. "Cultural Landscape Report," 24.
176. Ibid.
177. "[T]he new owners of the Ford house anticipated growing public demand for authentic furniture in historic houses when they accepted from the Ford family a large list of belongings which would normally, have been dispersed. From the earliest days, the founders of the Washington Association made certain that at least part of the house would be reserved for the display of relics." Found in Jacob, "Historic Structure Report," part I, "Ford Mansion," 12.

Chapter 6

178. William J. Murtagh, *Keeping Time: The History and Theory of Preservation in America* (New York: Sterling Publishing Co., Inc., 1988), 37.
179. "Integrated Cultural Resource Report," 85.
180. Ibid.
181. Jacob, "Historic Structure Report," part I, "Ford Mansion," 14.
182. Ibid., 4.
183. Ibid.
184. "Cultural Landscape Report," 31.
185. Jacob, "Historic Structure Report," part I, "Ford Mansion," 1.
186. Ibid.
187. Ibid.
188. "Integrated Cultural Resource Report," 87.
189. Ibid.
190. Jacob, "Historic Structure Report," part I, "Ford Mansion," 1.
191. Ibid., 17.

192. In his retirement, Verne Chatelain, the first NPS historian, reminisced about the founding of the Morristown Historical Park. The idea of a historical park, run by a national agency, in conjunction with local support, was something that Chatelain found remarkably unique. He commented: "[Morristown] was the point of departure in the development of the… separate historical program, because the Morristown program gave us a chance, first of all, to develop a new concept…the concept of a national historical park and using those great values at Morristown which had so much to do with the story of the American Revolution, we could not only apply the term National Historical Park to this area under the provisions of the act that Congress passed but we could administratively set up the kind of historical program for the first time that I had begun to feel was necessary. That involved, of course, having these areas first of all, under men trained historically to know what the legitimate objectives of the area ought to be, and then to work toward a realization of those objectives… From the outset at Morristown the people there, as well as myself, insisted that the direction of the program should be historical, and under trained historians to work clearly toward the realization of legitimate historical values." Found in Harlan D. Unrau, and G. Frank Williss, "To Preserve the Nation's Past: The Growth of Historic Preservation in the National Park Service during the 1930s," *Public Historian* 9, no. 2 (1987): 24.
193. "Cultural Landscape Report," 32.
194. Murtagh, *Keeping Time*, 33
195. Ibid., 37.
196. Ibid.
197. Ibid., 38.
198. Unrau and Williss, "To Preserve the Nation's Past," 19.
199. Charles B. Hosmer Jr., "Preservation Comes of Age: From Williamsburg to the National Trust, 1926–1949," *Bulletin of the Association for Preservation Technology* 12, no. 3 (1980): 23.
200. Ibid.
201. Ibid., 25.
202. Murtagh, *Keeping Time*, 37.
203. Ibid.
204. Jacob, "Historic Structure Report," part I, "Ford Mansion," 6.
205. Ibid., 7.
206. Ibid.
207. Ibid., 10.
208. Ibid., 12.

209. Ibid., 18.
210. Ibid., 1.
211. Melvin Weig, assistant research technician, summed up the overall approach to the issue of examining the mansion: "In general, it may be said that all structural features dating from the Colonial period, except where rot or decay made their replacement with new material positively essential, have been retained. Features which dated from after 1779–80, the date of Washington's occupancy and hence the period of greatest historical significance for the mansion, were removed and the original features restored, so far as research made possible, or replaced by features of appropriate Colonial design, as indicated by known examples of other Colonial architecture in northern New Jersey. A very few concessions to modern needs have been made to accommodate heating, plumbing, and electric and telephone systems." From Jacob, "Historic Structure Report," part I, "Ford Mansion," 1–2.
212. "Cultural Landscape Report," 32.
213. Ibid., 34.
214. Ibid.
215. "Integrated Cultural Resource Report," 198.

Afterword

216. Ibid., 81.
217. Ibid., 80.
218. Ibid.
219. Ibid., 81.
220. Ibid., 82.
221. Ibid., 83.
222. Ibid.
223. Patricia West, *Domesticating History* (Garden City: Doubleday & Company, Inc., 1996).

A Note on Sources

224. Guter, "Historical Data Investigation," CRBIB #012351. The document was found in the research files of the park library. Guter explains on page two that the study he conducted "was meant to evaluate

the extent literature devoted to the house, to assess the contents of sources discovered or put in better order subsequent to the last investigation and to summarize the value of the total documentary package."

225. Ibid., 5.
226. Ibid., 6.
227. Ibid.
228. Ibid.
229. "Integrated Cultural Resource Report," 194.

Bibliography

Some items are listed as draft. There are two reasons for this: one, the drafts were never finalized due to budgetary constraints; and two, in some cases the drafts were logistically easier to work with physically due to their slimmer nature. The narrative portions of the draft versus the final product did not differ.

Primary Sources

Ford Family Papers, Morristown National Historical Park Archives.

Gerlach, Larry R., ed. *New Jersey in the American Revolution, 1763–1783: A Documentary History*. Trenton: New Jersey Historical Commission, 1975.

Historical Magazine. "A Brief Account of the Province of East-New-Jersey, in America." Private reprint of copied article, Morrisania, New York, 1867.

South Carolina Historical Magazine XIII, no. 3. "Diary of Timothy Ford, with notes by Joseph W. Barnwell." (July 1912).

Secondary Sources

Archdeacon, Thomas J. *New Jersey Society in the Revolutionary Era*. Trenton: New Jersey Historical Commission, 1975.

Bushman, Richard L. *The Refinement of America: Persons, Houses, Cities*. New York: Alfred A. Knopf, 1992.

Cunningham, John T. *New Jersey, America's Main Road*. Garden City: Doubleday & Company, Inc., 1966.

Dalzell, Robert F., and Lee Baldwin Dalzell. *George Washington's Mount Vernon: At Home in Revolutionary America*. New York: Oxford University Press, 1998.

Fiske, John. *The American Revolution*. Boston: Houghton, Mifflin and Company, n.d.

Gerlach, Larry R. *The Road to Revolution*. Trenton: New Jersey Historical Commission, 1975.

Marling, Karal Ann. *George Washington Slept Here: Colonial Revivals and American Culture, 1876–1986*. Cambridge, MA: Harvard University Press, 1988.

Murtagh, William J. *Keeping Time: The History and Theory of Preservation in America.* New York: Sterling Publishing Co., Inc., 1988.

Pulinka, Steven M. *Discover the Historic Houses of Odessa*. Winterthur, DE: Henry Francis du Pont Winterthur Museum, 1999.

Ryan, Dennis P. *New Jersey's Loyalists*. Trenton: New Jersey Historical Commission, 1975.

———. "Six Towns: Continuity and Change in Revolutionary New Jersey, 1770–1792." PhD diss., New York University, 1974.

Sweeney, John A.H. *Grandeur on the Appoquinimink: The House of William Corbit at Odessa.* Newark: University of Delaware Press, 1989.

Thayer, Theodore. *Colonial and Revolutionary Morris County*. Morristown, NJ: The Morris County Heritage Commission, 1975.

Wacker, Peter O. *The Cultural Geography of Eighteenth Century New Jersey*. Trenton: New Jersey Historical Commission, 1975.

Zinn, Howard. *A People's History of the United States.* New York: HarperPerennial, 1980.

ARTICLES

Hosmer, Charles B., Jr. "Preservation Comes of Age: From Williamsburg to the National Trust, 1926–1949." *Bulletin of the Association for Preservation Technology* 12, no. 3 (1980): 20–27.

Unrau, Harlan D., and G. Frank Williss. "To Preserve the Nation's Past: The Growth of Historic Preservation in the National Park Service during the 1930s." *Public Historian* 9, no. 2 (1987): 19–49.

NATIONAL PARK SERVICE STUDIES

Arbogast, David. "Inventory of Structures." Cultural Resources Management Study No. 14, Morristown National Historical Park, 1985.

Craig, Vera B., and Ralph H. Lewis. "Furnishing Plan for the Ford Mansion (1779–1780)," Morristown National Historical Park, 1976.

"Cultural Landscape Report for Washington's Headquarters, Morristown National Historical Park." Vol. 1, "Site History." Draft. Boston, MA: National Park Service, Olmsted Center for Landscape Preservation, 2002.

"Cultural Landscape Report for Washington's Headquarters, Morristown National Historical Park." Boston, MA: National Park Service, Olmsted Center for Landscape Preservation, 2005.

Guter, Robert P. "Historical Data Investigation: The Jacob Ford Jr. Mansion, Washington's Headquarters." Prepared for the Morristown National Historical Park, Morristown, NJ: July 1983. CRBIB #012351.

Holland, Francis R., Jr. "Historic Structure Report." Part I, "Ford Mansion." Morristown, NJ: Morristown National Historical Park, 1959.

"Integrated Cultural Resource Report: Morristown National Historical Park." Amherst: University of Massachusetts, Archaeological Services, draft, February 2001.

Jacob, Judith M. "Historic Structure Report." Part I, "Ford Mansion." Morristown National Historical Park. National Park Service, North Atlantic Region, Cultural Resources Center, Building Conservation Branch, draft, October 1993.

Massey, William U. "Historical Grounds Survey of Washington's Headquarters, Ford Mansion." Morristown, NJ: May 1975.

"Morristown National Historical Park Cultural Landscape Report for Washington's Headquarters." Boston, MA: National Park Service, Olmsted Center for Landscape Preservation, 2005.

Racine, Laurel A. "Historic Furnishings Assessment." Morristown National Historical Park. Morristown, NJ: Northeast Museum Services Center, December 2003.

Wrenn, George L. "Historic Structure Report." Part II, "Architectural Data Section on the Ford Mansion." Morristown, NJ: Morristown National Historical Park, 1963.

WEBSITES

Academy of American Poets, "Haunted Houses." http://www.poets.org/viewmedia.php/prmMID/19993.

Partial Index

S

W

About the Author

Photo by Sarah Minegar.

Dr. Pfister has been at Morristown since 2004 and has been with the National Park Service in the field of historic preservation and cultural resource conservation since 1993. Prior to 1993, he worked for the Delaware State Archives. Dr. Pfister oversees the museum, archival and library programs at Morristown and has as his goal the integration of the separate disciplines into a single unit representing our cultural heritage. He has experience in a variety of curatorial settings affecting many of our nation's most important historic sites and collections. His professional interests include American constitutional development; the development of American historiography as a separate discipline; historic preservation and the communication of cultural patrimony to the general public; and understanding the broad scope of historic preservation through the interconnection of cultural resources. He earned his BA from Delaware State University in 1991, his MA from Washington College in 1993 and his doctorate from Drew University in 2007. He is the author of *The First Decade of the United States Supreme Court* and several articles.